MW00578517

**What People Are Saying About *Sobrietease* and
*Sobrietease 2: Make It a Double***

"Martha Carucci is one of those extraordinary individuals whose spirit defies words. Her strength, self-awareness, ability to dig deep, compassion for others and commitment to transformation of herself and the world around her is amazing. I love Martha's spirit and tenacity. I love her grace. I love how her light lights up those around her. This is another great read and I know you'll enjoy and be touched by her words as much as I have."

—Maimah Karmo, bestselling author, speaker, transformational coach, and cancer survivor

"As intensely personal as its message is universal, *Sobrietease* is exceptionally well written, organized and presented. As informative, thoughtful, thought-provoking, and ultimately inspirational, *Sobrietease* is unreservedly recommended for community library Self-Help/Self-Improvement reference collections and the personal reading list of anyone struggling with substance abuse—or has a loved one who is."

—*Midwest Book Review*

"We all face challenges in life, and how we choose to handle these can make us stronger. Martha handles her challenge with sobriety by combining humor, emotion, and honesty in her writing, making both herself and the reader even stronger."

—Susie Jackson

"Martha's writing is very much like her: engaging, approachable, charismatic, and real. Her humorous stories of life in sobriety have made me laugh and cry, often both at once. This book is a treasure trove of wisdom."
—Mary Bowers

"I've been a friend of Bill W. for thirty years. I have had two falls. I've been sober for twenty years. I read Mrs. Carucci's first book and was so impressed. I bought a few copies for friends. She is a warrior...and is courageously helping those who need it."
—Charles Zdebski

"I have known Martha as a fellow recovering alcoholic since she first got sober and I bought the first copy of the original *Sobrietease* from her. I love her candor and honesty, as all of us in recovery battle with our alcoholic minds that work to lure us back to drinking. Her writings reflect the reality of life in recovery."
—Bob Hisel, twenty years sober

"Finally, someone who knows what she's talking about."
—Anonymous

"Martha approaches her life as she does writing this second book—with humor and humility, with grace and honesty, and with the hope that she could help just one person who is suffering."
—Joanne Sawczuk

"Martha writes with honesty while sharing the good, bad, and ugly through her journey. She shares real-life experiences with her clever wit and raw inspiration. This book is sure to reach others who may not have wanted to reach out for help but feel Martha's story resonates in some way. Knowing they are not alone, her words may encourage them to reach out for guidance and support. Martha's writing is heartfelt and real. Martha is a dynamic, energetic, and thoughtful person and writer."

—Delia Sullivan

"Martha's writings and books have gone through important changes. She has recounted her memories and regrets of drinking into the dawn and how dark those days were. Martha then guided us on a journey of self-discovery through her sobriety. And though all those words and stories and chapters truly compelled me…I find this next chapter in her writing especially interesting. As she continues to commit to a sober life and the fundamental merits of this choice… she is no longer just speaking to counting the minutes one day at a time as an alcoholic. She is speaking to a drinking culture that has, more often than not, disappointed the human experience. She offers a view of what it feels like to live fully and without regret. It is an empowering look at the relationship with alcohol and how it may impact one's best self and deepest ability to create and live a fully empowered life. Thanks to Martha for sharing her gripping experience and wisdom."

—Nicky McDonnell

"Martha's commitment to sobriety expressed in writing is honest, raw, and oftentimes humorous. I stand in awe of her strength and look forward to continued inspiration by witnessing her living her best life and generously sharing her story."

—Mary Edwards

"Martha graciously allowed her readers into her daily life and shared her perspective with her successful blog and publication of *Sobrietease*. She uses even more of her wit and gritty honesty in this second book. Martha is not afraid to share her every day struggles and the harsh reality of navigating the modern world of perpetual alcohol promotion and its influence on a recovering addict.

She has a vast number of readers, and all of us love and appreciate her."

—Kristen Britt

"I have walked hand-in-hand with Martha on my own journey of recovery, inspired by her honesty, courage, and insights. Martha is living proof that, by committing to working a recovery program one day at a time, we alcoholics can attain a measure of wholeness, peace, and joy we never thought possible."

—Kathy S.

sobrie ease
make it  a double

ANOTHER ROUND OF MUSINGS ON LIFE WITHOUT BOOZE

martha carucci

www.mascotbooks.com

Sobrietease 2: Make It a Double

Author photo by Delia Sullivan

For more information, please contact:
Mascot Books
620 Herndon Parkway, Suite 320
Herndon, VA 20170
info@mascotbooks.com

Library of Congress Control Number: 2020911070

CPSIA Code: PRV0820A
ISBN-13: 978-1-64543-087-2

Printed in the United States

This book is dedicated to the amazing angels who:
-opened the doors for me
-walked beside me
-waited patiently when I couldn't quite keep up
-told me to slow down and breathe
-pushed me when I needed it
-pulled when I was stubborn
-knew when to listen and when to speak
-loved me when I couldn't love myself
-believed in me when I didn't
-laughed with me
-wiped away my tears
-let me go to use my wings
-brought me back down to land on my feet
-wouldn't let me take shortcuts but insisted I do the work
-helped me find my voice
-reminded me to use it
-taught me about grace, faith, and hope
-never gave up on me but continued to show me the light...
 and send the sunshine

Table of Contents

Introduction

On May 28, 2012, I decided to take back control of my life. For so long, it was lost to the bottle. The day that I began my journey into sobriety and recovery, over seven years ago, changed my life for the better.

In February of 2013, I started blogging anonymously as "SoberMom." While the writing was very cathartic, it was so much more to me than just a cleansing release. I wanted to share my story to help others. To let people struggling with alcoholism or addiction know that they were not alone. To help to minimize the stigma associated with the disease. To show the world that alcoholism doesn't discriminate; it will infect anyone, including the suburban mom sitting next to you at a PTA meeting and cheering in the bleachers at their kid's soccer game.

I started writing about my experiences as I battled those difficult "firsts" without a drink: my first sober holiday, my first sober party, the first stressful situation I had to handle without alcohol, etc. I talked about how my sobriety affected my relationships with family and friends. I talked about what I learned from others who had many more years of sobriety under their belts, and I tried to share some of that wisdom.

In what I like to call a "God wink," a local pastor sat next to me on the bus ride during our sons' field trip. We started talking and our conversation somehow led to me sharing my story with him. I was aware that he spent a lot of time doing prison ministry, and I was very interested in eventually working with incarcerated women. A few weeks later, he asked if he could interview me for a sermon he was preparing for his congregation. He said he could simply play the recording of my voice and I could remain anonymous. I told my husband about this opportunity, and my jaw dropped when he said, "If you feel so strongly about helping other people who are struggling with this disease, why don't you forgo the anonymity?" The pastor played the interview without revealing who I was. He simply referred to me as his "friend."

However, still thinking about my husband's comments and blessing, I talked to my oldest child, who was 12 at the time, and asked her thoughts on my being open and public about my alcoholism. I asked her what she would say if one of her friends said something to her about her mother being an alcoholic. Would she be embarrassed? Ashamed? She paused for a brief second and simply responded, "I would say my mom used to drink. A lot. But she doesn't anymore, and I'm really proud of her." That was about all I needed to hear. I sat down to write a brief piece I called "Coming Out Party," and revealed to the world that I was, in fact, SoberMom. I was completely overwhelmed by the support and encouragement I received. I kept writing, tackling a wide range of issues as a sober mom, friend, wife, daughter, and woman.

I published my collection of writings in April 2016, and that first book, *Sobrietease*, was the #1 New Release on Amazon for Alcoholism and Recovery books. Once I made the decision to share my story to help others, I welcomed the opportunities to spread the word to even more people. I did numerous television and radio interviews and podcasts, was featured in multiple publications, gave talks about the book, and responded to the outpouring of questions and requests for help from friends, neighbors, acquaintances, and strangers for either themselves or someone they loved who struggled with alcoholism. There were days when I thought about giving up, when I thought about picking up a drink, but I stayed strong, thanks to my support network and my Higher Power (HP). I continued to write, and I share what I learn as I continue on my journey through recovery and sobriety and into a much better life. One day at a time.

Now, over seven years sober, I continue to grow, change, and learn in my recovery. There is so much more I want to share with anyone who struggles or loves or cares for someone who battles the disease. I hope you find something in here that helps you or someone you love. We all have our crosses to bear, and it's never too late to turn things around. *Sobrietease 2: Make It a Double* is about continuing to fight the fight and find serenity. Enjoy.

Martha

Relapse or Renew

There have been several times in my recovery when I heard someone share about relapsing. One would think that the agony on the person's face and the guilt and shame they relate would be enough of a deterrent to anyone ever picking up a drink again. I've heard from people who have been sober for years and years who have swallowed their pride and admitted to their fellow alcoholics that they "went back out." It's always so tough to hear and to watch them suffer. And it's always one hell of a wake-up call and reminder that we can never get too complacent when dealing with this disease.

Recently, however, one person's relapse hit me quite hard. I went to visit a friend who was recovering from major back surgery. She was remarkably strong and in relatively good spirits considering her situation. She had expected to be convalescing in her home under the loving care of her partner of many years, but she was there alone, having to fend for herself and rely on friends and neighbors to bring groceries and meals. Unbeknownst to my friend, her partner, who had been sober for 24 years, had started drinking again a year ago at Christmas. She was not there to help my friend in her recovery from her surgery because she was in the hospital herself, fighting for her own life because her liver was failing. She had done so much damage to her liver by drinking so heavily 24 years ago that by picking up again, she went right back to where she left off. There's a reason that alcoholism is described as "cunning, baffling, and powerful."

No one in their right mind would choose to do something to themselves that would cause one of their major organs to stop functioning. That's just it—she wasn't in her "right mind." Apparently, over Christmas last year, this woman had been around friends who were drinking, and that evil little drink devil reared its ugly head and made her think that she should be drinking, too. Just one drink couldn't hurt, she must have thought. But that's never how it works, is it? Not for an alcoholic. It may not be the first time you pick back up. You may be able to have just that one drink. But inevitably there will be more. And more. Until you drink yourself to death. Literally.

I'll spare you the details of what is happening to her body physically. Suffice it to say, it's not pretty. I can only imagine what is going on in her head emotionally. Fear? Guilt? Shame? Remorse? Regret at not being there for her partner who needs her now? Anger at this horrific disease? A disease known by so many, but a disease with such a huge stigma attached to it still. So, what does my friend say when people ask where her partner is? How about that she is in a battle for her life, up against a most formidable foe? Why is there so much shame surrounding the disease of alcoholism? It's not something we brought upon ourselves. Yes, how we choose to deal with it is something that we control, but we didn't catch this disease. We weren't careless or weak. We didn't let our defenses down and somehow acquire it. Yet most people are quite reticent to admit to anyone that they are an alcoholic.

I choose to admit it freely for several reasons. It's my hope that by putting myself and my story out there, I can somehow help others who are suffering. I used to be horrified at the thought of anyone finding out, but as I said, it's a disease. It's not a weakness. It's not a lack of willpower or self-control. People need to learn about it and need to try to understand as much as they can. Chances are very good that you may know someone who is an alcoholic. But think about it: If you ever told someone else about them, did you whisper when you got to the part about them being an alcoholic? Maybe you didn't want anyone else to hear the embarrassing word.

I want people to know that they are not alone. I want them to know they should not feel ashamed. I want to pass on what has worked for me to keep me sober. I want other alcoholics to know that it is in fact possible to fight this disease and win. Relapses can happen, and given the recidivism rate for alcoholism, they happen quite often. But a relapse doesn't have to mean failure. You can get back up and return to the right path. You can renew your quest for sobriety and a better life. Fear, guilt, and shame can be replaced with bravery, determination, and pride. But we can never sit back and rest on our laurels. That opens the door for the cunning disease and the evil little drink devil. It requires constant vigilance and work. For many, it's an everyday battle. For my friend's partner, it's a battle for her life. If you are an alcoholic, think of her the next time you want to pick up a drink. If you're not an alcoholic, please say a prayer for her. You don't have to whisper.

Easter Miracle

O n this particular Easter Sunday, I choose to focus more than ever on the miracle that Easter represents. The miracle of Christ rising from the dead. Not just rising from the dead, but ascending after a horrific and brutal, yet incredibly symbolic, crucifixion. As the Bible says in Isaiah 53:4, "Surely He has borne our griefs, and carried our sorrows: yet we did esteem Him stricken, smitten of God, and afflicted." He bore our sins, our diseases, our sicknesses, and our pain for us so that we may live free forever.

On this particular Easter Sunday, I remember that verse as I pray for a sweet little boy who was in a terrible car accident a few days ago. His mother, who is strong in her faith, reminded her friends that life can change in an instant. But as she sits in the ICU with her son, her faith grows even stronger. It is quite possible that someone would look at this situation and ask, "Why?" Why, if Jesus bore our pain and grief, would this happen to an innocent child? I ask the same question about another dear friend's daughter who has a tumor on her spine that she battles with chemotherapy and possibly surgery. Why would a just God allow this to happen?

On this particular Easter Sunday, I have many more questions than I have answers. And yet, I find my faith growing stronger as well, inspired by my friends who handle these situations with the utmost grace and faith. I don't know that I would be able to handle such difficult, trying times as well as they do. I pray that I won't have to. And I feel helpless, sitting on the sidelines, unable to do anything for them. But I can do something. Something important. I can pray. I can pray to the God who sacrificed his only Son for us, the Son who bore all our sickness and grief on the cross, for hope, health, and healing. And I can believe, as I do with all my heart, in the power of prayer.

On this particular Easter Sunday, as I attend church with my family, I give thanks for all that I have, especially health. And I pray. I pray for my friends and for their children. I pray for my friend whose partner is suffering from the grave repercussions of her alcoholism. I sing and remember why we celebrate Easter. I rejoice in the miracle that Easter represents. That Christ has risen from the dead. That miracles do happen. I turn to my faith more than ever. And I have the utmost faith that God will take care of all His children.

"The true miracle is not walking on water or walking on air, but simply walking on this earth."
—Thich Nhat Hanh

Once I Was 20 Years Old

I'm on a train on my way to Philadelphia for my 25th college reunion. I can't even fathom the concept of having graduated 25 years ago. I just don't feel that old. While I'm very excited to see old friends on my former stomping grounds, I have a bundle of nerves wrapped up in my stomach. But I've already got one huge God wink to embrace and I eagerly anticipate more.

I'm going to see my old roommate and best friend whom I haven't seen or talked to in 20 years. We had a very stupid falling out a few years after we graduated and never spoke again. I barely remember the conversation, as I was well into my first, if not second, bottle of wine while we spoke on the phone. Many times over the years, I thought of what it would be like if I ever saw her again. What would I say? What would she say? Would she still be upset with me? She was like a sister, and we did everything together. I became part of her family and traveled with them. She and I went cross-country when we graduated from college and enjoyed numerous adventures together. Memories that will never be forgotten, despite what happened.

I have thought of her often over two decades but have no idea where she was or what she ended up doing. Enter the age of social media and the opportunity to track anyone down quite easily. I tried a few times to find her and eventually came up with a phone number on the Internet, but chickened out on getting in touch with her. Several months ago, what should pop up on my Facebook page but a friend request from her. I took a deep breath and clicked "confirm." We started sending messages back and forth via Facebook. Then moved on to emails. Then texts. Neither one of us held a grudge or mentioned what happened, but rather moved on and picked up the friendship pretty much where it left off.

Here's the God wink: I told her that I was sober now and had stopped drinking almost four years ago. Her response? "Welcome to the club." She had 13 years of sobriety under her belt. As much as I am looking forward to the reunion this weekend, I can also see it as a HUGE threat to my sobriety. There was a whole lot of drinking in college. On every corner, a bar I used to frequent, a fraternity house where kegs of beer flowed, a friend's dorm room where we partied. It's pretty much a miracle I graduated on time with a degree.

There is a big dinner party tonight for our class and with the tangle of nerves in my stomach at the thought of walking into the twilight zone, I'm comforted by the thought of going with my sober friend. In the past, a situation like that would scream "get a drink" to me. I would orchestrate my plan for immediately heading straight to the nearest bar for a large pour of liquid courage. This would be a really tough weekend if my friend were still drinking. It would be way too tempting for me to resort to old, alcoholic behaviors and go back to partying like the old days. People, places, and things that are triggers are killers for alcoholics. I'll have them all wrapped up in a nice bow for me this weekend.

But the old days are just that. These are the new days. I'm going back to a place in time and memory. I don't have to go back to the same actions and behaviors. People change and grow, and over these last four years of sobriety, I've grown more than any other time in my life. I'm guessing that with 13 years of sobriety, my roommate has changed and grown quite a bit as well. As have many other classmates, I'm sure.

I'll also get to see my book displayed at the school bookstore along with those of other alumni authors. It feels very surreal to me, but I worked so hard with my awesome publishers and editor to get the book finished in time for this weekend. I never would have thought 25 years ago that I'd return to college having written a book. I never would have thought 25 years ago that I'd be dealing with alcoholism. And I never would have thought just four short years ago, in the throes of a wretched disease, that I'd be walking onto my college campus again, with my head held high, a happy, proud, recovering alcoholic. Or with my long-lost roommate, back together again for new adventures and memories.

"An old day passes, a new day arrives. The important thing is to make it meaningful: a meaningful friend – or a meaningful day."
—Dalai Lama

A Wild Ride

One of the things I didn't anticipate in sobriety was the vividness of the feelings I would experience once I no longer numbed myself with alcohol. The last few weeks have had me on a roller coaster of emotions, and the ride continues now as I begin another journey. I wish I could say I was traveling just for fun, but I'm not. That was last weekend when I wrote about heading to my 25th college reunion in Philadelphia.

I'm now on a plane to Houston where I will meet up with my best friend and her two children. Her daughter is having surgery at one of the top cancer centers in the world to remove a tumor that has been decimating her upper spine. It's a major operation with a great deal of risk involved. So once again, I have a knot of nerves in my stomach: eager anticipation of the removal of the malicious growth in her body and return to her "normal" life, and fear of complications or potentially dreadful outcomes. But I can honestly say that the positive thoughts for a successful surgery and recovery far outweigh the fear. Why? Prayer and faith. Not only my own, but lots from those who surround this girl and her family with love.

In my last post, I wrote about the bundle of nerves I felt while on a train to Philadelphia for my reunion—nervous anticipation of seeing my former roommate and closest friend after 20 years of not speaking, fear of difficult tests of my sobriety as I would be surrounded by people, places, and things that were all major triggers of my drinking, and nostalgic yearning for the "old days," when I was 20 years old and before the demons of alcoholism reared their ugly heads.

The weekend was wonderful. My roommate and I managed to pick up right where we left off, both agreeing to leave the past behind us and move forward with our friendship. We stayed up until almost 3 a.m. reminiscing about numerous hilarious adventures together. We walked the campus where we roamed confidently and carefree 25 years ago and saw familiar faces and classmates that have grown much older. I got to spend time with three other close friends and enjoyed catching up with them immensely. I was thrilled to see my book in the university bookstore in the section with other alumni authors, humbled to even be associated with most of them. And proud of myself for making it through the whole experience without the need to pick up a drink. Nervousness, fear, nostalgia, humility, and pride were enough ingredients in my emotive cocktail for the time being.

I got on the train home, intending to write a follow-up blog piece, but was far too tired. I actually managed to doze off for a bit. The emotional roller coaster can be exhausting. I got off, spent a week at home with my family (a wild ride in and of itself), and just got back on for another go. Twenty-thousand feet up in the air, my current concoction is one of fear and anxiety mixed with awe at my friend's grace and bravery as she faces this ordeal, gratitude for the opportunity to be there with her and her children, and appreciation of my faith and my new-found ability to let go and let God, and to turn over the things that I can't control.

Oh, and I can't forget, thankfulness for my sobriety, which affords me the ability to be strong for someone who has been a rock for me every step of the way on my journey. Please pray that this ride comes to a happy stop.

Love and Laughter

There's a reason why my tagline is "God, grant me the serenity to laugh at life." In critical situations, what are the choices? Tears or laughter?

I know people talk about families coming together in times of crisis, but the family I was with this week did more than just come together. Facing an extremely risky surgery to remove a tumor from her spine, my best friend's 14-year-old daughter carried herself with grace and bravery leading right up to the surgery. The risks and danger of the procedure were explained to us. All the pertinent questions were asked. But there was laughter. Lots of it. Sure, some of it may have been nervous laughter, but it was jovial and comforting to all. In fact, my stomach actually hurt from laughing so hard.

What was the alternative? Allow anxiety, stress, and worry to take over? None of those things would do anything to improve the outcome of the surgery.

And then came the waiting. And the waiting. Eight hours into the surgery and still waiting. But with the waiting came more laughter. I was amazed at my friend's ability to stay calm and wait patiently for updates every two hours. Any nerves and anxiety were quelled by the fact that not only is she in the hands of some of the best surgeons in the world, she is in God's hands. As I wrote in my last piece,

I'm learning to "let go and let God." I'm also learning that as much as I may sometimes think I should be able to, I can't control everything and everyone all of the time. And as much as I joke that everything is about me, I really do get it that this isn't about me at all, but is about some pretty spectacular people.

I'll repeat a quote I've used before: *"If it's sanity you're after, there's no recipe like laughter."* —Henry Rutherford Elliot

Stay tuned.

Health, Happiness, and Healing

O nce again, I'm in transit as I write. I'm on a plane on my way home from Houston. The roller coaster is rounding the bend and coming to its last downward slope. For this turn on the ride, at least. It was, as I anticipated, a wild ride full of loops. I'm exhausted, physically and emotionally, and if I am this tired, I can only begin to imagine how my friend feels after her daughter's surgery and the past few, very difficult days of recovery.

First off, the surgery was successful. The doctors managed to remove the tumor intact and she was wiggling her toes soon after she woke up. We all cheered as those happy little dancing toes were moving, indicating that one of the major fears surrounding surgery on her spine had been eliminated. And then came more laughter and joy. As she began to talk more, we saw the effects of the drugs and anesthesia as she asked repeatedly for a duck and then for someone to bring her 92 bags of ice from a gas station. Her mouth was so dry, but she wasn't allowed to have anything to drink yet. Finally, she got some ice chips and managed a faint smile. During the last few days, I've realized that sometimes the little things in life make all the difference in the world.

It wasn't all laughter and calm the last few days, though. Following the surgery, she was in terrible pain and, despite all the different medications they tried on her, she couldn't seem to get any respite. Two horrible nights for my friend and her daughter, awake all night with the staff trying to manage her pain and difficulty breathing. Fear that something wasn't right since the pain was that unmanageable. Sure enough, they did an X-ray and found a small tear in the pleura of her right lung and it was pooled with blood. They inserted a chest tube, and then a second one, to drain the lung, and finally she got some relief.

Yesterday, she managed to get out of bed a few times and even took about 20 steps with the aid of a physical therapist. Unbelievable to me so soon after major surgery. Last night brought more breathing difficulty though, and when they finally got her more comfortable and back to sleep, it was time for me to go. I wanted to stay, but much more importantly, I wanted to let my friend get some sleep while her daughter was resting. While the thought of leaving them there was gut-wrenching, my heart was more at peace knowing that she was on her way to recovering, hopefully closer to her normal life than she has been. I put on my big girl panties and my poker face, and hugged my friend goodbye. She's one of the strongest people I've ever met, and while I know that she would have been fully capable of dealing with this all on her own (as she is accustomed), I hope that by being there I helped somewhat. I got on the elevator, and as the doors finally closed, I let the tears flow. A lot of emotions bundled up in the past few days. It's one thing to watch someone you love suffer. It's another thing entirely to witness someone you love watching their own child suffer and not being able to do anything to comfort them.

I got up at 4:30 a.m. for my flight and realized the irony of the fact that exactly four years ago today, at about that same time of morning, I sat on a street corner in NYC with the same friend and finally got the words out to her that I was an alcoholic. I'm looking forward to getting my four-year chip this week at my home group meeting. I even made it to a recovery meeting in Houston yesterday. In another ironic twist, the building in which I attended the meeting was named after a huge donor whom I had known years ago in the heyday of my drinking.

So now it's time for me to head home to my crew, to whom I am very grateful for managing without me for a week and whom I missed very much. I have no idea what kind of shape my house will be in when I return, but having been through what I have this week, I honestly don't care. Health, happiness, and healing are really all that matter.

"You know, all that really matters is that the people you love are happy and healthy. Everything else is just sprinkles on the sundae." —Paul Walker

Float Like a Butterfly, Sting Like a Bee... "The Greatest" Kissed Me, Playfully

With the recent passing of Muhammad Ali, I thought that I would share my story about my encounter with "The Greatest." For my first job out of college, I worked at a trade association in downtown Washington, D.C. My new boss, some of my coworkers, and I were having lunch in a conference room that had windows facing the front of the building. As we ate our lunch, we noticed a small crowd gathering outside in front of the bank across the street. As the "new girl," I was sent to go see what was going on.

When I got outside, the mob was gradually growing, and I could finally see what the excitement was all about. Muhammad Ali and the small entourage that accompanied him had just come out of the bank. He was very noticeably shaking from his Parkinson's and for some reason, I caught his eye. He proceeded to basically play "hide and seek" with me, hiding behind the columns outside the bank. He would peek out, smile at me, and then go behind the column again. This repeated a few times and then he motioned for me to come closer. Meanwhile, the throng of people watched this exchange curiously. I myself was wondering what it was all about. Why me? I walked toward him as he requested, and he leaned forward and kissed me on the cheek. I must have turned a ridiculously bright shade of red. After that, the Champ and his crew got into a car and drove away.

I wondered if my coworkers saw this whole exchange from the windows. I eagerly ran up the stairs, threw open the door, jumped up and down and said, "The Champ kissed me!" To say they were jealous is an understatement. Being the new girl that day had its advantages. The man whom many consider the greatest athlete of all time kissed me on the cheek. For no apparent reason. I guess there was a reason though—to give me a story to tell my kids... and you.

On the Road Again

Once again, I find myself on a train...this time heading to NYC for the weekend with my daughter. We are going to spend the weekend with her godparents who have an apartment in the city. Shopping, a show, and super restaurants. Can't wait.

So, while on the train, do I do some of my recovery work or do I write a blog piece? I guess you can tell which one is winning. Can you say procrastination? One of the things I have to work on is a list of some of my character defects and things I would like to change in myself. Many people have a very hard time looking at their own character defects and digging into the past, often uncovering numerous demons. I've known a few people who have never been able to do this because it is just too painful to face.

But when we look at our character defects, we are also supposed to look at our assets. So when an alcoholic looks at their "moral inventory," we must consider not only our defects, but also our assets. For many, this can be hard as well, if we have a hard time finding the good qualities in ourselves due to low self-esteem, among other things.

I'm not going to list all of my character defects or assets here. But I will say that it's obvious that procrastination is a big defect of mine. And perhaps when it comes to doing this exercise, fear. If I knew exactly what I was afraid of, I might be able to deal with it better, but it will take some digging. Some digging that I keep putting off. I know that there are many things that led me to drink, and many things that I regret having done while drinking, but a big part of recovery is forgiveness and moving forward. As they say, "We do not dwell on the past nor wish to close the door on it." We revisit the past and learn from it what we can, and then move on.

In the past four years of sobriety (I'm coming up on 1,500 days next week, but who's counting?) I've learned so much. I've done a great deal of soul-searching and introspection. There's a lot that I saw that I didn't like, but also some that I did. We should all take the time to see our good qualities. A friend in recovery calls me "AG" for Atta Girl. I'm a firm believer in patting oneself on the back when it's called for. In my case, those days and nights I make it through a rough craving without picking up a drink. Or when I have a major breakthrough of understanding or come to a great revelation about myself or my drinking. On some days, I literally give myself a pat on the back just for getting out of bed.

I've had a few reasons lately to be both displeased with myself for some of my actions, but also proud of myself for trying to correct them. Overall, I'm going to give myself an "Atta Girl" pat on the back. Sometimes I'm a little slow, but as long as I learn from my stupidity and mistakes, it's not so bad. I've also got a few amazing people in my corner who I can always count on for a kick in the head when it is called for instead of a pat on the back. Believe me, often that's what I need. Everyone should be so lucky to have friends who care enough about them to kick them in the head sometimes.

Not sure if being nostalgic falls into the character defect or asset column, but I'm coming up to that part of the train ride when we pass by my old alma mater in Philly. I can see the stadium and high-rise buildings and even some of my old haunts as the train passes by. I was just there a few weeks ago for my 25th college reunion (see my piece called "Once I Was 20 Years Old"). My daughter says she would love to go there one day. Raising smart kids—that definitely falls into the asset column.

For more nostalgia, I'm going to see one of my oldest and dearest friends tonight. She and I were actually in incubators next to each other in the hospital when we were born (just a few days apart). Really looking forward to seeing her. Keeping in touch with old friends—asset.

And I can't make a trip to NYC without being hit with the memory of it being the city where I had my last hurrah when it came to drinking. Memorial Day weekend, four years ago, my hands shook until I got a drink in me at lunch. Not this time. Sober and happy to be able to remember every minute I get to spend with my daughter and dear friends. Progress—asset.

Now on to my recovery work...

"God has promised forgiveness to your repentance, but He has not promised tomorrow to your procrastination." —Augustine of Hippo

The Fortress of Solitude

I have a friend who has shared with me a little about what it was like growing up with alcoholic parents. After hearing some of her stories, I am so grateful that my children will grow up with a recovering alcoholic and not one still actively drinking. She is one of the smartest and most generous people I know, which is all the more impressive knowing the circumstances under which she was raised.

Unfortunately, she's packing up to move a few hours away. Although I'm sure we will keep in touch, I will miss our tea time together, often several times during the week. I'll also miss her as a confidant, loyal advisor, and wonderful friend. The friend who introduced us also moved away, and she is sorely missed.

Back to the alcoholic upbringing. The few stories she has relayed to me are horrific. She was pushed down the stairs and left temporarily blinded by her mother when she was in an alcoholic rage. Often times, when her mother started drinking and Mrs. Hyde's appearance was imminent, my friend would hide inside a small, round table in their house. Her mother would never find her in there and would become even more infuriated.

As my friend is packing up her belongings, she is getting rid of a huge amount of "stuff" since they are downsizing considerably. The time has come to decide what happens to the round table. The Fortress of Solitude. The Safe Haven. To those who might look at it in an estate sale, it would just be a normal table, suitable for putting drinks or little knick-knacks on. To her, it carries a whole treasure trove of memories.

Alcoholics are cautioned to avoid people, places, and *things* which may be triggers to their drinking. But what about things that just trigger difficult memories for someone who isn't an alcoholic? Do you hang on to those things because they hold so much meaning or let them go to try to alleviate the pain that they can bring? Packing up the "stuff" that you have accumulated over the years can bring a barrage of memories and past experiences. Perhaps that's why I have so many boxes of crap up in my attic. Too much to go through. Or perhaps too difficult to go through because of some of the memories associated with the "stuff."

A move is an emotional upheaval. The prospect of a new start is exciting, but the sadness at what you leave behind can be tough. I haven't moved much in my life—I've been in the same area for over 25 years. While a move would be good in that it would force me to go through all the stuff in the attic, I think I have had enough change in my life the past four years while getting sober.

Everyone has "stuff" and baggage from the past. How they sort through it and deal with it is a very personal. Lately, I've been sorting through a past of intangible items—my character defects that led me to drinking and the repercussions of my actions. Slowly but surely, I'm working through them and trying to become a better person for doing so.

As for the Fortress of Solitude, my friend has decided to let it go. Hopefully she will let go of some of the pain along with it. We may have scrapbooks of memories in our attics or simply in our minds. Maybe in the corners of our minds, as the song goes. They are no less real than the table. My friend can put a price tag on the table and sell it. The memories that go along with it have no monetary value, but the feeling of letting them go: priceless.

"There comes a time in your life when you have to choose to turn the page, write another book or simply close it." —Shannon L. Alder

Finding (and Using) My Voice

hicken: noun meaning "coward." When I drank, I did a really good job keeping everything inside and swallowing my feelings with each gulp of alcohol. The more things that piled up inside, the more difficult it was for me to use my voice. I never wanted to rock the boat, and I hated confrontation. I still do. When I got sober, part of what I needed to work on was finding my voice again and using it.

We are all born with a voice or some means of expressing ourselves. As children, we were fully capable of asking for what we needed and conveying our feelings. Sometimes they came across in the form of crying or screaming or stomping our feet. "I want an Oompa Loompa NOW, Daddy!" We didn't take into account how these outbursts would be received. We didn't care if they hurt someone else's feelings. That was a foreign concept to us then.

As we grew, we started to learn that our words and deeds affected those around us. There were repercussions to our tantrums. We began to realize that our words had the power of making other people feel good or bad. We even learned that sometimes our words carried the ability to come back and haunt us. Once we opened our mouths and spoke the words, we couldn't rein them back in. Today, with social media, this is even more true. I try to tell my kids that once they put something "out there," it's out there for good.

The good thing about constantly working on my sobriety is that I can see when I start slipping back into old habits. I realized recently that I was letting things build up and not using my voice to communicate my feelings. It's often easier to sit at the keyboard and type away rather than having to talk to someone face-to-face. That's not necessarily the best approach. Sometimes you need to be able to see someone's reaction to what you say—body language, facial expressions, etc.

I often wish that I were more assertive. I respect people who are. People who are able to clearly state and stand up for what they believe and what they need. Don't get me wrong, I've come a long way since I got sober. It's easier to see what's important with a clear mind. It's a little bit ironic, though, to talk about losing my voice while I was drinking. Many times, alcohol gave me the liquid courage to say things I probably shouldn't have. But most of the REALLY important stuff got gulped down or temporarily washed away with the booze.

Lately I realized that I had built stuff up to create a humongous problem in my mind instead of tackling it head-on. Chicken. Afraid of what result my words would have. Would they hurt someone else's feelings? Would I regret something that I put out there that I couldn't take back? This is where self-worth comes in. Believing that I am worthy of expressing my feelings, believing that how I feel and what I think are actually important. And they are.

I finally did use my voice. And things went very well. Better than expected. I could have saved myself a great deal of stress and anxiety if I had just opened my mouth sooner.

But I'm getting there. Stronger every day that I am sober. Wiser every day that I have a clear mind. Braver when I acknowledge that I am worth it.

> *"Be bold enough to use your voice, brave enough to listen to your heart, and strong enough to live the life you've always imagined."* —Unknown

Red F@%$* Solo Cups

There's something about early evening at the pool. The light is just a certain peaceful way as the sun goes down. The kids are still holding on to their last remnants of energy, hopefully expending what's left playing in the pool with friends. But this time of day is also when they come out in full force. The red Solo cups. The adults at the pool are having their end-of-the-day-beginning-of-the-evening libations in red plastic cups. Instead of concealing their contents, red Solo cups are like, well, red flags for alcoholic drinks.

I never noticed them before. Probably because I would have had one in my hand, too. It's just a tough time of day. At the beach, it's just as bad, if not worse. I think about coming home, wiping the sand off, and starting the blender. I probably would have already had a few beers down at the beach. I miss that. But as I've said before, I don't miss what came with it—ridiculous, drunken behavior, bad choices, and massive hangovers.

It wasn't always that bad though. There were definitely times when I wasn't over-served, as they say. When I just had enough to have a happy buzz. I'm sure I was more talkative and outgoing then. When is the line crossed? When does it become too much? I wish I could tell you. For everyone, it's different. For me, I could go from zero to stupid in about 30 minutes. And then that warm fuzzy feeling came and the slurring started. Much more babbling. And everything around me started to look better.

Something bad didn't necessarily happen every time I drank. But, pretty much every time something bad happened, I had been drinking. As an alcoholic trying not to pick up a drink again, I can't look back at the "fun" drinking times and romanticize them. If I'm going to stay sober, I have to remember the times that too many red Solo cups led me down the wrong path.

We're at a friend's house at the beach now, and I can tell you that I'm trying hard to remember why I don't drink. I'm surrounded by alcohol as I type, with no one around right now to know if I picked up or not. But I would know. And HP would know. I won't do it. I am determined to make it to day 1,538. So what do I do? I call my support network. I pray for more strength. I remove myself from the situation. I look out at my boys playing in the pool and remind myself why I am sober today. Without my sobriety, I wouldn't notice the beautiful light this time of day. I wouldn't look out on the water as the boat cuts through it and think optimistically about the future.

For those of you who can drink a nice cocktail out of your red Solo cup, cheers and enjoy. I'm going to go make myself a mocktail and look at the water. Perhaps I'll try a blue cup... and make up a new song to go with it.

The End of the Affair

I had an affair. A tawdry affair that lasted years longer than it should have. It could have destroyed everything. Several people's lives could have been ruined. Even worse, I carried out my affair in the open, for all to see. I was seduced at a young age and the romance grew. It took all I had in me to gather the courage to break it off, but my love affair is finally over. The sultry, sexy, stimulating liquid that once gave me a warm glow and made me feel amazing (albeit temporarily) is no longer a part of my life. The break-up was years ago, but I still think about my love affair with alcohol.

Many of you can relate to that warm feeling that comes with drinking. The fuzzy buzz that comes after the first few sips. The warmth, comfort, and escape. But as is the story with many alcoholics, it usually goes downhill from there. I became completely dependent on the feeling that the booze brought, seeking it out at any cost. It was destroying my life until I was able to get a grip on it and accept the fact that the truth would set me free.

The truth has set me free. The truth is that I am an alcoholic. It was an affair that was destined for disaster. It's out in the open now and I share my story willingly in hopes of helping others avoid the pain. Don't start the affair. If you do and feel it's gotten out of control—that the affair has taken over your life—break it off. If you need help to do so, get it. It's out there and available.

Many of you know the story of my affair. You may even relate to it a little too well. The drinks that are fun at first. That help you relax and unwind. That help give you the liquid courage to walk into an otherwise uncomfortable or intimidating social situation. That you can't wait to pour at the end of a long day. That you seek out first thing at a party.

But do you know the ones that you start to crave earlier and earlier in the day? The ones that you seek to make you feel a little better after a rough night—the hair of the dog? The ones that you don't just want, but must have? The ones that you start to hide because they are becoming too numerous? The ones that temporarily put an end to your hands shaking? These are the ones that often make the affair more insidious and dangerous.

The first step is admitting that your life has become unmanageable and that you are powerless over alcohol. The affair is notorious for this. After the seduction by the powerful temptress, alcohol takes over your life. Your thoughts are consumed by where and when you are going to get your next drink. When you will be with your lover again.

For many, the affair with alcohol has destroyed their lives. They kept it up at huge costs. They may have succeeded in keeping it hidden, but most often they can't. Those close to them usually find out. In my case, many knew. Some expressed their concern and others even tried to talk me out of it. I'm incredibly blessed that I didn't have to face a horrific rock bottom. I came close to losing a great deal, but thanks to a tremendous amount of love and support, the break-up occurred before too much damage could be done.

My life is so much better now that the affair has ended. My husband and my family know that I have moved on, and I have made my peace. The temptation is still there occasionally, but I am stronger. I am no longer so easily seduced. I know the dangers of the temptress. I know the seductive singing of the Sirens in the form of a deep red bottle of wine...and I can now turn my sails in another direction.

"It happened this way: I fell in love and then, because the love was ruining everything I cared about, I had to fall out." —Caroline Knapp, *Drinking: A Love Story*

God Bless Us, Everyone

I haven't had much time to write lately and now that the chaos of the holiday season is upon us, I'll probably have even less time. But once again, I was on a train up to NYC and finally sat still long enough to catch my breath and have some time to reflect. I also haven't had much time to get to meetings and I can definitely feel it. I start getting squirrely. We're heading into a very tough time of year for me, and for many alcoholics, and more meetings are crucial to make it through the holidays sober.

Thanksgiving has always been tough for me. It was a day of heavy drinking and some memorable meltdowns. I would start drinking pretty early in the day as I prepared the food and set the table. A walk over to our neighborhood football game was usually good for a few Bloody Marys or mimosas. Plenty of wine with dinner and the flow continued well after dessert. I still remember the embarrassing drunken episodes. But there will be no more. This was my fifth sober Thanksgiving. I will hit four and a half years of sobriety on the 28th. And life is SO much better.

I have numerous things for which I am very thankful. Too many to list here, but suffice it to say that I thank God every day for my sobriety and for all I have. I think you tend to appreciate what you have much more when you come close to losing it. In the height of my drinking, I was on a path of destruction that could have caused irreparable damage. Many people have asked me at what point did I know that I was an alcoholic and had to get help to stop drinking—when I reached my rock bottom.

I am one of the very fortunate alcoholics whose rock bottom doesn't have a horrific story. Don't get me wrong, it was pretty awful for me and those around me, but not nearly as bad as some of the stories I have heard in the rooms. While many accounts may be similar, everyone has his or her own rock bottom.

One of the best descriptions of rock bottom I have heard during my sobriety is when you realize that the thing you lost last or the next things you are about to lose are more important to you than alcohol.

For me, the next things I was about to lose were more important to me than booze—my family, friends, health, sanity, and more. It just took me a long time to realize it. Had I not, things would look very different for me this holiday season, if I was even still here to enjoy it.

And, thanks to a wise friend, I'm learning to look forward optimistically rather than back regretfully. The past is the past. I can learn from it, but move on and look forward to new Thanksgivings and holidays rather than dwell on the pitfalls of past. It's a good time of year to take stock of what is truly important to us and not let booze, or anything else, put us at risk for losing it. Whatever your demons are that can take you down, it's never too late to get help and turn things around.

Happy belated Thanksgiving and warm wishes for the holiday season upon us. I hope you can realize and appreciate all your blessings, too. Don't wait until you risk losing them to do that.

"Reflect upon your present blessings—of which every man has many—not on your past misfortunes, of which all men have some." —Charles Dickens, *A Christmas Carol and Other Christmas Writings*

Happy Holidays!

Like many people, I've found myself consumed with holiday activities and preparations and with little time to write. This piece will be brief—I just want to wish you all a very Merry Christmas, Happy Hanukkah, or anything else you may be celebrating. Thank you for all your support and kind words throughout this year. They really mean a great deal to me.

As tempted as I've been to pick up a drink throughout this chaotic season, I can't. And I won't. I just spent some time with my youngest child tracking Santa on the computer. Sober. I wouldn't trade that for anything. I'll wake up early tomorrow morning to see the excitement on my kids' faces and I won't have a massive hangover. I'll remember the conversations we have over Christmas Eve dinner tonight. And, I'll celebrate day 1,672 of my sobriety tomorrow, as well.

I'll try to get another piece out soon. Meanwhile, stay warm, safe, and strong.

M

"Christmas waves a magic wand over the world, and behold, everything is softer and more beautiful."
—Norman Vincent Peale

Time May Change Me, But I Can't Trace Time

On Facebook, I just saw a tribute to the many talented people we lost this year—David Bowie, Prince, Muhammad Ali, Carrie Fisher, George Michael, Gary Marshall, Florence Henderson, Glenn Frey—and the list goes on. At the end of every year, there is a nostalgic look back at the major events and passings. This year, there seems to be an exceptionally large number of them.

The lyrics of David Bowie, Prince, George Michael, and others were often beyond brilliant. Many of Bowie's songs were quoted by teenagers filled with the angst and the pains of their days. "And these children that you spit on as they tried to change their world, are immune to your consultations, they're quite aware of what they're going through" was a quote I referred to often in high school. Prince's *Purple Rain* album also brings back memories of high school, as our team colors were purple and white and our soccer team used to sing the song as "Purple Reigns."

Florence Henderson will always be Mrs. Brady to me. Gary Marshall gave us *Laverne and Shirley, Happy Days,* and other iconic shows. Muhammad Ali was "The Greatest" and, as I have written before, kissed me on the cheek one summer day nearly 30 years ago.

Yes, time has indeed changed me. I am a completely different person than the one I was just five years ago thanks to my sobriety. I didn't just stop drinking—I completely changed who I am at the core. In order to get sober and STAY sober, one must get down to the very root of what led to the drinking in the first place. Why the need for an escape? The need to be numbed? Did that teenage angst lead to the bottle? Did the family of origin fall far short of the Brady bunch and result in not-so happy days?

Glenn Frey crooned in "Desperado": "Your prison is walking through this world all alone." During the last few years of my sobriety, I've learned how to break out of that prison and that I don't have to walk alone. I have an incredible support system and for that I am truly blessed. I just received a call last night from a friend in between flights while traveling clear across the country to see if I was doing okay and give me a pep talk to get through the holidays without picking up a drink. He's on my gratitude list.

George Michael never knew how right he was when he sang, "Maybe we should all be praying for time." It goes quickly. Take the time to enjoy it. To be real. To be present. To be grateful.

*"Dearly beloved we are gathered here together
to get through this thing called life."* —Prince,
"Let's Go Crazy"

I'm Still Standing

Most of my readers know how much I like to quote song lyrics. One of my favorite Elton John songs is "I'm Still Standing" and recently, my boys have started singing it around the house because it was featured in the animated movie, *Sing*. It's a great, upbeat song that says:

> *Don't you know I'm still standing, better than I ever did.*
> *Looking like a true survivor, feeling like a little kid.*

That can mean so many different things to people, for whatever their struggle is. For me, it's alcoholism. Sometimes I need to remind myself that I have been triumphant in my struggle and despite its power over me, I'm still standing strong. I've been picking up the pieces of my life for several years now (actually 1,706 days, but who's counting) and although I can't say it's without alcohol on my mind, it's on my mind less frequently than when my journey into sobriety began.

I'm still standing after struggling to get through the holidays sober, surrounded by alcohol at a number of parties and events. I'm still standing after some rough personal trials and tribulations. I'm still standing after years of battling depression. During the more difficult times, I rely more heavily on my recovery network, and I am truly grateful for their help. They make sure I'm staying strong and check on my emotional sobriety. Basically, they make sure I'm still standing.

For me, the "still standing" also has a very literal meaning. My go-to escape throughout my battle with alcoholism and depression has been hiding in my bed, isolating. While it's not a great way to handle things in life, it's definitely better than what my escape used to be—alcohol. On days when things are rough, I want to just pull the covers over my head and hide, and I often do. But once again, I'm incredibly grateful to my support network and close friends who will pull me out, sometimes literally, sometimes just with a text, and let me know I need to get up and face the world and live my life. You can't look like a true survivor buried under your covers. It's the opposite of still standing. I could write a song that says I'm still hiding, but I'm not sure that would go over very well and it certainly isn't very inspirational.

Whatever your struggle may be, give yourself a pat on the back for standing strong. Some days you may just have to be proud of yourself for getting out of bed. It's a good start. We all have our times when we don't feel like we have the energy or strength to stand tall. And it's okay to hide sometimes, but life goes on around us. It's better to participate in your own life, even when times are tough, than to let it pass you by. Stand strong.

"Be sure you put your feet in the right place, then stand firm." —Abraham Lincoln

Welcome to Fantasy Island

Do you remember the television show *Fantasy Island*? A white-suit-clad Ricardo Montalbán and his trusty sidekick, Tattoo, greeted a planeload of guests at the beginning of each episode. They came to the island to live out their fantasies. I was recently reminded of this show as someone pointed out to me that I may be trying to live in a fantasy world of my own these days.

Let's face it. The real world is tough. Really tough. Who doesn't want an escape occasionally? For me, the escape used to come from the bottle. So now that there's no bottle, what is my escape? Those of us with addictive personalities usually find something to replace whatever it is that we are addicted to. Some people start smoking. Some become exercise fiends. Some turn to Ben and Jerry's, candy, and other sugary treats. Some find vices that are even worse.

But at the end of the day, the real world is still there. We may think the grass is greener somewhere else or in a different situation, but when we are sober and present in our lives, we are able to use the tools we have to make the best of the reality. I'd rather feel the ups and downs than be completely numb.

Drinking was like a mini-vacation to Fantasy Island. It was an escape from reality, but it often ended in a nightmare. Blackouts, massive hangovers, throwing up, bad decisions, etc. Whether we wanted to or not, somehow we were always on the return plane. We woke up. We got over our hangovers with either time or with the hair of the dog. The real world was always there when we came back.

One thing that helps me deal with the real world now is the Serenity Prayer, which I try to remember to use often. "God, grant me the serenity to accept the things I cannot change, the courage to change the things I can, and the wisdom to know the difference." The fact is, in the real world, the majority of things we think we have control over are things we cannot change. Just pause to think about that when you are in a troubling situation. If it isn't something you can control, turn it over. Let it go. Leave it to your Higher Power to handle.

For the things we can change, sometimes we do indeed need the courage to take the necessary steps to do so. Change can be very difficult, especially for those who take comfort in the status quo. Taking bold steps to make necessary changes is hard. Being sober is a huge change. It takes strength and courage to put the bottle down and figure out a new way to escape reality when need be. A healthy way. But for now, I'm signing off to have some Cherry Garcia. Stay strong.

"If one is lucky, a solitary fantasy can totally transform one million realities." —Maya Angelou

How Big is the Damn Onion?

Peeling away the layers of the onion. A common phrase heard in recovery rooms and plastered all over self-help books. Stripping away the surface layers, getting to the core of the problem. After almost five years of sobriety (God willing, I'll hit that milestone on May 28) and peeling many, many layers of the onion, I have started to wonder when I'll ever finish peeling. Or *if* I'll ever finish peeling.

In order to achieve and maintain sobriety, you have to take a hard look at the things that led you to drink in the first place. Some of these are obvious. Some come after peeling back layers of the onion. Just like when you peel a real onion, peeling the metaphorical onion can lead to tears.

It's hard work. And usually not fun. There are things that we all wish we could forget. And sometimes we do forget them. For a while. And then they start bubbling up to the surface. We peel back the layers to reveal them. Often painful memories. But with the peeling comes growth. Working through the layers and getting to the root of things may be painful, but it can facilitate a great deal of personal growth and betterment.

It seems like my journey into sobriety and recovery has been nothing but peeling away the layers of the onion. The peeling goes hand in hand with working the twelve steps. Starting out with admitting that we were powerless over alcohol and that our lives had gotten out of control, we throw away the crutches of the booze and rip off the surface band-aids with one fell swoop. It is the ultimate first peel of the onion and waving of the white flag. But there are often deep scars underneath the bandages. And yes, you guessed it, the more we peel and unravel the bandages, the deeper and deeper we get.

The peeling continues when we take a moral inventory of ourselves. That's some serious peeling—taking a look deep inside yourself and recording both your character defects and your personal assets. Often, it's the listing of the assets that is more difficult for people. Why do most of us find it easier to point out our faults rather than shine the light on our strengths? Human nature?

Then we get to share the peeling process. We share our moral inventory and our deepest secrets with someone we trust implicitly. Ouch. This part feels pretty damn raw. It feels like we are completely exposing ourselves, and it is the ultimate moment in vulnerability. Then we turn our attention to those whom we have harmed. This step takes more soul-searching and memory bank withdrawals. So if you've been waiting for an apology from me since I got sober, get ready. And if you don't get one, it means that perhaps I haven't peeled back enough layers of the onion to remember what I may have done to you that merits an apology.

We learn to continue to take personal inventory at the end of every day and immediately face and own up to our wrongs. Just when you thought you had all the fun taking personal inventory, you get to do it again. Digging deeper. Peeling more layers away. But the exercise leads to a great deal of freedom. Promptly admitting we are wrong about something allows us to learn from our mistakes and move on quickly. And to grow.

It is our hope that peeling the layers of the onion brings us closer to the God of our understanding. We are reminded to pray for help and to meditate in order to connect with our Higher Power, both allowing us to dig deeper to get to the core of the onion. We hope for a spiritual awakening. Does the spiritual awakening come once we have peeled away all the layers of the onion? Have we reached the core and lightened our load? Are we done?? No. I'm not sure we are ever done. We continue to evaluate, assess, take inventory, see where we can do better, apologize, and move forward. I know I have a long list of shortcomings. But I also have a long list of assets. As I mentioned, let's not just beat ourselves up for our character defects, but give ourselves a pat on the back for our strengths when we do all this work.

I believe the onion is pretty damn big and that it takes a great deal of hard work to get to the core. But it is possible to get there. And maybe, just maybe, what you find at the core isn't so bad. Or if it is, hopefully you have built up your strength through all this hard work and have found solace in your prayers and meditation to handle it. And if you have had a spiritual awakening, you're in even better shape.

Peeling the layers of the onion and working the steps aren't easy tasks. But they are so worth it. We get rid of what we no longer need. We get rid of the guilt. We let go. We allow the good stuff to come in. Peel away the layers and open your heart and your mind. So how big is the damn onion? As big as your life.

"Life is like an onion. You peel it off one layer at a time and sometimes you weep." —Carl Sandburg

Cinco de Derby

Cinco de Mayo Friday. Kentucky Derby Saturday. To me, that used to mean margaritas and mint juleps. Not anymore. I just hit 1,800 days of sobriety. A good friend pointed out, ironically, that 1,800 is also a tequila. So, cheers to those of you enjoying those drinks, and cheers to me.

There was always a reason to drink. For me, it used to be just because it was a day that ended in "y." Or Arbor Day—there's cause right there to celebrate. The Ides of March also brought an excuse to party. You name it—I could find a reason to drink. I was depressed, so I thought a drink would help make me happier. I was stressed, so I thought the drink would take the edge off. I was frustrated, angry, resentful—whatever—and always thought a drink would make it all better. It might have provided some temporary relief and distraction, but it never made things better. Usually quite the opposite.

But this year, I didn't pull the covers over my head and hide from these occasions like I did early in my sobriety. This year, I went to a good friend's birthday party on Cinco de Mayo and a Kentucky Derby party on Saturday. A few years ago, I wasn't able to do anything of the sort. Was there drinking at both parties? Yes. But the wonderful thing for me was that being surrounded by alcohol didn't really bother me. I had my own special drinks and enjoyed them. I could actually relax and not be overcome with anxiety about the temptation. Progress. Lots of progress.

I know that I have to be grateful for the progress, which comes with a great deal of hard work, but not get too cocky. I need to remember what it used to be like. The miserable hangovers, the forgotten nights (and days), the drunken screw-ups. It is often referred to as "the gift of desperation." We remember what brought us to admit our alcoholism and to get help. And became *willing* to accept our powerlessness over alcohol and the fact that our life had become unmanageable.

I went to a meeting almost every day this past week. Meetings help keep me grounded. Often it is too easy to let life get in the way of working on my sobriety. I can't do that. Without my sobriety, there is no "life" to get in the way.

I gave a talk at our public library last week. I was touched by many of the people who came out to hear it and support me. Despite the fact that the talk ended on a very positive note, one woman, whom I have known for many years, was in tears. She said it was hard to hear all that I went through and that she couldn't believe she didn't know or realize my struggle while I was in the middle of it. I've heard that from several people. I guess I was pretty darn good at putting on a happy face. But now you see the real me. Hopefully you see a humbled, grateful, and genuinely happy recovering alcoholic.

Three weeks from today, God willing, I will be celebrating five years of sobriety. Memorial Day. And the weekend before, I'll be in NYC, where I found my "gift of desperation" on the street corner at 4 a.m. There's a big reason right there to celebrate. Sparkling cider for everyone is on me.

"The gift of willingness is the only thing that stands between the quiet desperation of a disingenuous life and the actualization of unexpressed potential."
—Jim McDonald

Just a Little More

You may have heard the recent news about the death of Soundgarden lead singer, Chris Cornell. While the story is still unfolding, his death was reportedly a suicide by hanging. Cornell was only 52 years old and a recovering addict. His family is questioning whether the drug Ativan played a role in his death. Cornell had a prescription for the anxiety drug, but may have exceeded the recommended dosage. The possible side effects for the medication are suicidal thoughts and impaired judgement. Was it the addict in him that led him to take "just a little bit more" for added benefit? Cornell went public about being newly sober with the help of Alcoholics Anonymous in 2003. He remained clean and sober for many years. And then this. A tragic, preventable death.

But what you didn't hear about in the news was the passing of a lovely, elderly woman who battled alcoholism for decades. I had the privilege of meeting her and getting sober while having her experience, strength, and hope to guide me. She was an animated Southern belle who imparted great wisdom with her deep Southern drawl. Her death brings sorrow and grief to those who knew and loved her, but there is also a certain amount of peace surrounding it because she died a sober woman. She fought the "cunning, baffling, and powerful" disease for decades.

And won. I'll always remember her humorous stories and infectious laughter.

So the contrast? A famous lead singer in a popular rock band. A little-known, elderly Southern woman. Two completely different worlds. Suicide vs. natural causes. The common factor? Addiction. Supposedly both recovering alcoholics/addicts. Vastly different people bonded together by sharing the same disease. I guess Cornell's toxicology report will shed some light on whether or not he was, in fact, still in the throes of his addiction. Regardless, I pray for both of their families and that they both rest in peace.

The death of famous actors or musicians tends to raise awareness about addiction, temporarily at least. But what about the millions of "normal" people who battle the disease valiantly out of the limelight but succumb to its power? Their passing isn't plastered on newspapers and magazines or online publications. Some die on the streets a horrific, lonely death without anyone even knowing. Not sure if that is worse or if being the loved one having to watch someone die from alcoholism is.

This isn't one of my more upbeat blog posts. But it needed to be written. The death of an addict, famous or not, serves as a good reminder of why we fight the fight every day. As has been said many times, alcoholism is "cunning, baffling, and powerful." It takes strength and determination to win the fight. It takes discipline. It takes HELP. If you need it, ASK for it. Many recovering alcoholics or addicts, including myself, take prescription drugs for anxiety, depression, or other things. We need to remain diligent and not let ourselves go to that place where we may think "just a little more" will help. Cross-addiction is something that we hear about all too often.

When I drank, it was always "just a little more." Just one more drink. Just a little more wine. Just another shot. And it always led to just a little more trouble. Now, it's "just a little more" in a much different way. Just a little more time without a drink. Just a little more serenity. Just a little more strength. Just a little more help from my Higher Power. There are many things for which more is better. Alcohol and drugs aren't examples of those.

I'm in NYC this weekend celebrating my upcoming anniversary of five years of sobriety. Back to the last place where I had a drink, Memorial Day weekend of 2012. I am so much stronger than I was back then. So much more grateful. And honestly, I'm just a little prouder.

> *"Talent is God-given. Be humble. Fame is man-given.*
> *Be grateful. Conceit is self-given. Be careful."*
> —John Wooden

A New Way of Living

When I was younger (much younger), I used to eagerly count down the days until my birthday. I couldn't wait for my special day when the sole focus was on me and I would anticipate all of the presents I would receive. Okay, maybe I'm not so different today. Today, I counted up my days of sobriety, 1,826 to be exact, and I reached my five-year anniversary. Or five-year birthday, as many in recovery like to call it.

On your "regular" birthday, you celebrate the fact that you were born. Let's face it—you didn't do much. Your mother did all the work. But it marks the day you came into this world. Your sobriety anniversary or birthday on the other hand, marks the day your new life began. A better life. A second chance. Something you did have a huge role in. It celebrates the choice you made to live.

My emotions run the gamut today, but what I feel mostly is gratitude. I think about the last drinks I had in NYC on Memorial Day weekend five years ago. I think about how awful I felt when I woke up, how my hands shook until I had a drink in me. I think about how ashamed I felt when I admitted I was an alcoholic. I think about how insurmountable the concept of getting sober seemed. And I think about how much better I feel now that I am sober. How proud I am of the fact that I didn't pick up on the many occasions when I felt like caving. How grateful I am to those who stood by me and helped lift me up when I needed it.

I'm very happy to have my shiny, new five-year coin. But I am also trying to remember my need to stay humble and strong. This disease is cunning, baffling, and powerful. Today is just another day in the battle. It's always there, ready to pounce. I'm still just a second away from picking up a drink and going back to the insanity. But as my sponsor says, it's okay to give yourself an "Atta Girl" every once in a while, and pat yourself on the back.

While I celebrate my special day, I am also painfully aware of the fact that there are so many out there still suffering. I wish I could somehow let them experience how I feel right now and let them know that they can get there, too. Yes, it's hard work, but it is oh so worth it. To my friends who are struggling right now, please try to stay strong. Life is so much better on the other side of this wretched disease. And it is a disease. It is not a weakness or a lack of willpower. Reach out for help if you need it. Turn to your Higher Power, whatever that is for you. For me, that Higher Power (or HP) is God. And I couldn't have done this without my faith in Him.

I heard at a meeting today that getting sober isn't about thinking your way into a new way of living, but living your way into a new way of thinking. I really like that. I am living a new way, without drinking, with much more gratitude and with a much stronger connection to my HP. Doing so has resulted in a new way of thinking for me. Thinking that life is good. Sobriety is wonderful. And each day is a gift. So, on to day 1,827.

And, God bless those who gave their lives for our country. Talk about gratitude.

"As we express our gratitude, we must never forget that the highest appreciation is not to utter words, but to live by them." —John F. Kennedy

Sober Cum Laude

It's graduation time. A time when so many young people move up and move on. Happy celebrations that mark one chapter in life that is ending and a new one beginning. I was delighted to celebrate some of these special occasions with dear friends recently and to be able to do so sober.

In the midst of the festivities, however, yet another friend in recovery went back out "to do more research." They fell off the wagon. They went back out to their old world of drinking. Often, the action is facilitated by one particular thought: "I've got this now." However long they have been sober—10 days or 10 years—they think that they can now "control" their drinking. Sorry to say, that ain't gonna happen.

If, however, you are able to prove me wrong, my hat is off to you. No one I know or have met in my five years of sobriety has been able to do that. In fact, I've shared some pretty heartbreaking stories on my blog about people who went back out and never returned—they lost their lives to the disease before they could get back into recovery. Once a pickle, you can never go back to being a cucumber.

But many people who go back out come right back in. They get themselves back into a recovery program immediately. We are all human. We make mistakes. This disease is cunning, baffling, and powerful, so kudos to those who get knocked down and get back up again. I hope that I won't find myself in that situation but...

Recovery is not a program from which one ever "graduates." But then again, neither is life. If we aren't constantly learning, we are going backwards. I can honestly say that some of the most important and most helpful things I've learned have been in recovery. And they are pretty basic things that can help anyone, alcoholic or not.

Sobriety 101 teaches us "one day at a time." Sounds so simple, but often so hard to live by. When I first got sober, the idea of never having a drink again, EVER, was completely overwhelming to me. What helped the most was when someone would remind me that I don't have to do it forever, just for today. Tomorrow is another day, and I will tell myself the same thing. In tough times, this may get changed to "one hour at a time." Make life manageable for yourself. Break things down into attainable goals.

We also learn another crucial axiom: "Do the next right thing." Again, alcoholic, addict, or not, everyone can use this reminder. When you come to crossroads, make the right choice. It's not always easy, believe me, I get that, but ask yourself what the next right thing is and find a way to do it. If you need to, ask for help.

In AP Sobriety, things get a little more complicated. We hear things like, "Change I must or die I will," "Attitude of gratitude," "Stinkin' thinkin,'" and, my personal favorite, "Turn it over." Again, all of these can be useful to non-alcoholics as well. Who doesn't have "stinkin' thinkin'" sometimes? Many of us could use an attitude adjustment, and we can all stand to have a little more gratitude. I realize that is very difficult when times are tough. That's where the "turn it over" part comes in. One thing I've learned on this journey of sobriety is to trust in my HP, my Higher Power. When things get really difficult, I have to remind myself to turn them over. Some things are bigger than I am, but not bigger than HP. Whatever your Higher Power, your spirit, your God, remember to turn things over to It/Him. I know that without my HP, I wouldn't be sober right now.

Whether you are in recovery or not, there are certain things in life that we could all use refresher courses in. Sometimes we just need to go back to basics, like the lessons above. I've had 1,854 days in sobriety school and I learn something new every day. Thanks to all of you who have taught me life lessons along the way. You have my attitude of gratitude.

"The aim of education is the knowledge, not of facts, but of values." —William S. Burroughs

How Big is the Damn Onion - Part II

Awhile back, I wrote a piece called "How Big is the Damn Onion." It was about working on ourselves and peeling the layers of the onion to get to the root of our issues. I'm revisiting this concept because I find myself with more layers peeling recently, and I don't really like it. Frankly, it scares me and I worry about my sobriety as some of these major layers peel away and lead to things I thought I had shoved down into my subconscious for good. Not deeply enough, I guess.

Today is the Fourth of July. A time when many people are getting out their red Solo cups (another piece I wrote a while ago) and there is a lot of alcohol consumed. I feel like I am totally surrounded by it. Tomorrow is my daughter's 16th birthday. I'm finding it stirring up a lot of things for me. First off, I can't believe how quickly time has flown since my life changed when I became a mother with her birth. It makes me think of my own 16th birthday and I REALLY can't believe how quickly time has flown since that day over 30 years ago. My mother managed to arrange a surprise party for me and gave everyone where I worked for the summer t-shirts to wear that said, "Martha is 16 Today!" I still have mine.

My daughter's request for her birthday was to celebrate it with two of her friends and me at the lake. A beautiful, serene place where we are enjoying time on the water and some simple things like making s'mores at a fire by the lake, getting ice cream, and just relaxing—something I don't do very often. But as I relax and unwind, I peel more of the layers of the onion away.

I had a bad drinking dream the other night. It was the kind where you wake up in a sweat thinking it was real. It was most likely prompted by a thought that came into my head about celebrating my daughter's birthday and not being able to toast her with some champagne. Same with her wedding someday. These are the times when being an alcoholic can frankly suck. But they are also the times when it is crucial to remember the simple saying: "One day at a time." When I first got sober, I was completely overwhelmed by the idea that I would never have a drink again. Some sober friends gave me excellent advice and reminded me that all I had to do was not drink for today. Don't worry about tomorrow or the future. I also remembered a friend telling me that she threw away her sobriety after one sip of celebratory champagne to toast her son's engagement. Her mistake became my lesson and, thank goodness, one that someone reminded me of the other day.

So I bought some sparkling cider and lemonade to toast with my daughter and her friends tomorrow. We plan to go on a hike by some local falls. We'll go back on the water in kayaks and canoes. I'll take some time to write and read. And I'll continue to peel back the layers of the onion. It's not easy by any stretch of the imagination, but as I wrote before, it's necessary to process things and then let them go. I've managed to do that with many things, but there are always more layers of the onion to peel. As a great friend pointed out, you'll probably peel away the last layer when you take your final breath in this world.

Happy birthday, America and happy birthday to my beautiful daughter. I'm glad I can celebrate both—sober and present.

The Power of Choice

B
ack in June of 2014, I wrote a piece called "Turn the Beat Around – Part II." It was the second blog piece I wrote about music and how so many songs revolve around drinking. At the end of the piece, I was talking about the song "Choices" by George Jones and I mentioned Dr. William Glasser's *Choice Theory.* I postponed a more comprehensive discussion about choice until another day. Well, today is that day.

As open and honest as I am in my writing, there's obviously stuff that is off limits and that I choose not to share here. Not now anyway. Maybe someday. Some of it is too embarrassing or shameful. Some of it would affect other people. Some of it I still need to process. Some of it comes as the layers of the onion peel away.

But as the saying goes, "You're only as sick as your secrets." So, I have to somehow get these things out and deal with them so I can move on and get healthier. It's not easy work by any stretch of the imagination, but it is vital. I'm not ashamed to say I go to therapy, I work with a sponsor, I work the steps of a 12-step program, and I am blessed to have a few people in whom I can confide, safely and without judgment.

In my last piece, "How Big is the Damn Onion – Part II," I talked about things bubbling up as I spent some quiet, contemplative time at the lake with my daughter. Stuff I had buried down into my subconscious. There's a show called *Hoarders,* where they follow people who accumulate tons of stuff over the years and then can't get rid of it. Their houses are completely filled from floor to ceiling with stuff. I think I am an emotional hoarder. I hold on to so much crap that I don't need. Not only do I not need it, it's harmful baggage. I don't want to be sick with secrets so I am *choosing* to let them go.

Dr. William Glasser, the psychiatrist who developed "Choice Theory" stated that "it is almost impossible for anyone, even the most ineffective among us, to continue to choose misery after becoming aware that it is a choice." Sounds simple, but maybe not. How can it be impossible to choose misery if your life is falling apart? Besides, I suffer from depression. I don't choose to be miserable...sometimes I just am. So, I started doing some more digging on happiness and choice.

There's a book called *The Happiness Project* by Gretchen Rubin. The subtitle is *Or, Why I Spent a Year Trying to Sing in the Morning, Clean My Closets, Fight Right, Read Aristotle, and Generally Have More Fun.* She spent a year chronicling her quest to be happier. She gives the reader tips for different monthly focuses geared to helping achieve happiness.

A friend told me today about another book called *Resisting Happiness* by Matthew Kelly. Its tag line is "A true story about why we sabotage ourselves, feel overwhelmed, set aside our dreams, and lack the courage to simply be ourselves...and how to start choosing happiness again!" I've already ordered it and am very curious to find out why I sabotage myself and why I "resist" happiness. Well, maybe I used to, but as I said, I'm choosing not to any more.

Now, five years into my recovery, I'm finally beginning to understand that everything is a choice, starting with my choice to get sober and healthier. Every day, I make a choice to stay sober. It is a daily reprieve based on our spiritual connection. I've been faced, many times over the past five years, with the choice to go ahead and pick up that drink or not. No matter how many days, weeks, months or years of sobriety I have, it can be gone in a split second with the wrong choice. Don't get me wrong, the choice isn't always so easy to make. Alcoholism is cunning, baffling, and powerful. It constantly tries to influence that choice in its favor. The Drink Devil vs. the Sobriety Angel.

As for the choice to be happy, I'm not sure it's quite that simple, but I am realizing that I have much more power than I thought. I **can** choose to do the next right thing, which can lead me to happiness. I can choose to let go of things which no longer serve me. I can choose to pile on the things I complain about or I can write a gratitude list. I can also let go of things I cannot control by reminding myself of the Serenity Prayer.

My message when I speak to people is that it's never too late to turn things around. First, however, you have to make the choice to do so. And, if somehow you don't know what the right choice is, ask for help or guidance. I'm guessing that deep down you may know the answer, but if you're like me, you've got too much old baggage to see clearly down there. That's why we say, "Let go and let God." Get rid of what no longer serves you and turn it over to your Higher Power. That's a huge step right there toward happiness.

I used to think I could find happiness in a bottle. I can tell you definitively that you cannot. I also used to think I could avoid unhappiness by pulling the covers over my head and hiding. That doesn't work either. Neither of those things allowed me to stand up and be present in my life. One of the most important pieces of advice I ever received is: If you make the choice to stand up and be present, things may not be easy, but you can look back and always feel like you gave it your best shot.

> *"Excellence is never an accident. It is always the result of high intention, sincere effort, and intelligent execution; it represents the wise choice of many alternatives—choice, not chance, determines your destiny."* —Aristotle

Feet in the Water

Wow. July 9 was the last time I wrote a blog piece. Thanks to everyone who has reached out. So much to say, but I don't know where to start. I feel like I did when I first started my blog in 2013—I didn't quite know where to start, but I knew that if I waited for the perfect time or for the perfect words to come, I would never begin. So, this isn't going to be a typical piece. It's really just for me to dip my feet back in the water, to let you know that I am still here, and that yes, I am STILL sober. One thousand nine hundred seventy-seven days sober. And that's nothing short of a miracle.

I don't have the energy to get into all the details, nor do I want to bore you with them, but I've been really sick for over three months. Exhausted, extremely weak, chest pain, difficulty breathing...was in the ER once and the hospital for a few days, as well. I've been to doctor after doctor, specialist after specialist, and have had more tests done and blood drawn than I can keep track of. I've tried traditional medical routes as well as alternative. I've done therapy, med evaluations, energy healing, massage, nutrition, and chiropractic. I've even changed the water I drink (which I'll have to explain in another piece). I'm down about 17 pounds and my entire body is just achy and weak. I could go on...

As frustrating as this has all been (and I still don't have any concrete answers), miraculously I haven't wanted to pick up a drink. And thanks to my sobriety, I have been able to look at all this and find some silver linings. I've learned a great deal about myself—emotionally and physically. I know that stress is playing a huge role in all of this somehow. And I'm starting to learn that I have to listen to my body and make some necessary changes in my life. I've been overwhelmed by friends who have been supportive, caring, and helpful. I've met some amazing people who have been through similar health issues and graciously shared their experiences and wisdom with me. I've let go of things that I simply can't do and am starting to set up some healthier boundaries. I've begun to practice what I preach and have reached out for help—not something alcoholics are typically good at. I guess basically this whole situation has made me really reassess what is and isn't important in life.

So there. It's a start. I know there is a reason I am going through this. I know I'll come out of it even stronger. I know how much writing has helped me in the past, so maybe just this small start is a step toward healing...

"Healing is a matter of time but it is sometimes also a matter of opportunity." —Hippocrates

One Day at a Time...2,000 Times

I posted on my Facebook page that tomorrow, Saturday, November 18, 2017, marks 2,000 days of sobriety for me. So, theoretically, tonight I should be partying like it's 1999. And I am—in my own way. I did a Facebook Live interview with my friend Holly Bertone/Pink Fortitude (http://www.pinkfortitude.com) about my book and tips for staying sober as the holiday season approaches. I hit a great meeting. And I had lunch with a very dear friend whom I have known for over 25 years.

It was so great to see her, but I wish it had been under different circumstances. Her younger sister just recently passed away after battling ALS. She was my age. ALS is an absolutely horrific disease that also took the life of my uncle a few years ago. We talked about her sister, her illness, the funeral, and about how everyone in her family was holding up. While there were some expected tears, there was a great deal of laughter. Despite the massive amount of grief my friend is enduring, she talked about her gratitude. Gratitude for her family, for her own health, and for the memories she will always have of her sister.

Gratitude has been on my mind a great deal lately. Yes, Thanksgiving brings a major focus on gratitude. It's been a topic in numerous meetings these days as well. It was even part of the lesson in my son's religious education class this week. And let me tell you, fifth graders have some awesome ideas about gratitude. For me, gratitude has truly been a gift of my sobriety. As I shared in my last piece, I've been dealing with some health issues. Things are far from perfect in my life yet somehow, instead of feeling the constant sense of impending doom that I used to feel, I am confident that everything will turn out okay. That serenity and trust is nothing short of a miracle.

Two thousand days is a miracle, as well. When I first started this journey, I didn't think I could make it two hours, never mind two days. Or 20. Or 200. But 2,000? Without a single sip of alcohol? Without turning to the bottle to numb the things I didn't want to feel? Without relying on liquid courage?

On this journey, I gave up drinking. I gave up a way of life to which I was accustomed. I gave up my known means of escape. But what I have gained has been immeasurable. I gained serenity. I gained humility. I gained self-respect. And, like I said, I gained gratitude. Or I guess it's more accurate to say that I gained the ability to be more grateful. Many friends I have met in my recovery are faithful about writing a gratitude list every day. For some, the items on the list can be as basic as having a roof over their head and food in their stomach. Sobriety took them off the streets and gave them food to put in their mouth in place of alcohol.

The things for which I am grateful are far too numerous to list here. Suffice it to say that I am grateful for the serenity that sobriety has brought me, in all aspects of my life. I am grateful for the ability to live my life being present. I am grateful for being able to learn from a friend who can laugh and be grateful even in dark times.

*"Let us be grateful to the people who make us happy;
they are the charming gardeners who make our souls
blossom."* —Marcel Proust

One Little Candle

I spent all last week in the hospital. I was admitted Sunday after a trip to the emergency room. Long story, and I'll spare you the nasty details, but I had a bad bacterial infection called C. diff. It basically tore up my stomach. I wasn't released until Saturday evening. Still on a strong antibiotic, quite weak and nursing my stomach, but very, very happy to be home.

No, it's not an ideal time to be down and out with the holidays here. But there's never really a good time to be sick. It is what it is. Christmas is going to have to be low-key this year. People will just have to understand. More importantly, I will have to understand. Which is hard. I'm used to going full speed and I just can't do that right now.

One of the most important things I've learned in my recovery is gratitude. I've written about it many times. One of my dearest friends always reminds me to find the silver lining in everything. I have miraculously been able to look at this whole situation and find the good. My family really rallied. The kids and my husband got the Christmas tree up and decorated, kept the house running, and lifted my spirits. My amazing sponsor spent almost every day with me in the hospital and showered me with TLC. Friends have been beyond generous with prayers, kind words, and dinners for my family.

My son's fifth grade religious education class that I teach made get well cards for me. I was blessed with an amazing assistant catechist whom I didn't know until this year but who has been an absolute angel. Just another example of how HP puts people in your life for a reason. She thoughtfully had the kids make cards for me and checks in often, as well. We also got a new student in our class just two weeks ago. A sweet girl who brought me a little candle for Christmas with a nice card. That simple gesture meant more than she or her family could have known. I had that candle next to my bed in the hospital, and it kept the room smelling like a Christmas tree. All the nurses and doctors who came in commented on it. It brought me a little Christmas cheer in an otherwise scary time.

The candle smells amazing. But it is also a symbol. A symbol of light. A symbol of hope. There's a song called "One Little Candle" which a couple of artists (Perry Como and Chicago) have covered. I think I sang it in chorus when I was in sixth grade. I found the lyrics:

It is better to light just one little candle,
Than to stumble in the dark!

This world could use a little spark and brightness right now. I know I could. Imagine if everyone lit one little candle and saw that candle as light and hope, too. Some friends light Hanukkah candles on their menorahs. Many will go to churches on Christmas Eve or Christmas Day and light a candle in memory of a loved one. I will light my little candle and remind myself to find the silver linings and my gratitude.

I'm grateful that the last thing I have wanted through all of this is a drink. My sobriety is truly a gift. I know this is a hard time of year for so many people who struggle with alcoholism, addiction, depression, and more. To them I say this: Have faith. Stay strong. No matter how bad things get, find something for which you are grateful. It may be as simple as a warm place to hang your hat. Trust me, it works. Just as a single little candle goes a long way, so does gratitude.

Best wishes to you all for a happy, healthy holiday season. Thanks for the continued support.

"Just as a candle cannot burn without fire, men cannot live without a spiritual life." —Buddha

Come from Away

I didn't anticipate writing a piece about one of the most tragic days in history as we just rang in the New Year and I optimistically look forward to good things ahead. But I saw a show in NYC last night that will forever change the way I look at September 11, 2001.

I knew very little about the show *Come from Away* going into it. I only knew that it was about the passengers on 38 planes that were diverted to a small town in Newfoundland on September 11 when airspace was locked down following the terrorist attacks in the U.S. I was curious and not quite sure what to expect.

I saw the musical with my daughter, who was barely two months old on September 11, 2001. Throughout the show, I was cognizant of the fact that we sat in those seats, just a short distance from Ground Zero, with two very different perspectives. She obviously doesn't remember that day, but as I looked around and saw the tears on the faces of the men and women around me, I knew they remembered it probably as vividly as I did. I felt a very strong connection to the complete strangers that I sat in that theater with last night.

In the small town of Gander, Newfoundland, the normal population of 9,000 almost doubled on September 11, 2001 when 7,000 passengers from 38 planes coming from all over the world landed there. The actors did a phenomenal job of captivating the stories of kindness and selflessness that the people in that small town exhibited over the few days they hosted these displaced, confused, worried, and exhausted travelers. They opened their homes, provided food and clothing, and put their own lives on hold to help people they had never met.

It was something I never knew and would have never thought about—the extent of the ripple effect throughout the world that the terrorist attacks had. It was impossible not to go back to that day in my mind. Sixteen years later, it's not something I think about often, perhaps only on the anniversaries. But I realized last night that there are so many people who probably think about that tragedy nearly every day as they either survived it, as did my brother-in-law who worked in Manhattan, or lost a loved one.

I still choose not to watch the documentaries or specials about that day. I can't listen to the recordings of the last phone calls. I don't want to see the bodies falling through the sky to the ground. My daughter shared with me that in her school, they watch the accounts of 9/11 every year on the anniversary. Students are given the option to leave the classroom. But that's all they have to go on. They were too young to know. I'll never forget watching the news that day in horror. Or hearing the jets soar over my house and seeing the smoke rising from the Pentagon, just a few miles away. I was due to return that week to my job as a lobbyist in downtown D.C. after my maternity leave, but I was crippled with fear and postponed it.

But time moves on. I eventually went back to work. The fear gradually lessened. But the world was forever changed. Ironically, one of the things I remember just a few days after the attacks was my daughter's godmother coming to visit us on her birthday, September 14, which she shares with my husband. She wanted to see and hold her goddaughter. She held a very high-level position in the U.S. government and the long days and nights and brutal amounts of stress at work following the attacks were taking their toll. Holding an innocent child in her arms during that time provided a brief respite of comfort. And here we were now, sixteen years later, visiting her in NYC and treated to the show as a Christmas gift from her. A gift that made an enormous impact on us both. I walked back from the theater with my daughter with tears rolling down my cheeks, a very rare thing for me. She even said to me that it was okay to cry. Yes, it absolutely is.

I was recently in a meeting where we talked about the idea that bad things happen in life, but good things can come from them. This show was an excellent reminder of that. There are so many stories from that day, many that we will never know, about both heroic acts and simple acts of kindness. There is a scene in the musical where many of the travelers, of all different faiths and backgrounds, go to a church and sing the Prayer of St. Francis, one of my true favorites. A very dear friend, an incredibly talented musician and healer, sang it and played the guitar to it at a meeting once. It was a gift to those of us in the room that day, and it was a gift last night as it moved me to tears and taught my daughter a wonderful prayer she didn't know. For those of you not familiar with the Prayer of St. Francis of Assisi, here it is:

Lord, make me an instrument of your peace,
Where there is hatred, let me sow love;
Where there is injury, pardon;

Where there is doubt, faith;
Where there is despair, hope;
Where there is darkness, light;
Where there is sadness, joy.
O Divine Master, grant that I may not so much seek to be
consoled as to console;
To be understood as to understand;
To be loved as to love.
For it is in giving that we receive;
It is in pardoning that we are pardoned;
And it is in dying that we are born to eternal life.

The people in the small town of Gander, Newfoundland gave all those things freely those few days following the attacks—love, pardon, faith, hope, light and yes, even joy. They consoled the weary travelers without regard for their own needs. I wish everyone could see *Come from Away.* I am so grateful to have seen it. To have seen it with my daughter. To have let my tears flow freely. To have been reminded of the kindness and good that exists in our world. To have sat next to total strangers and shared a moment in time. To have enjoyed a show on Broadway in a city that not just survives, but thrives. And to be 2,047 days sober and able to feel and express the gratitude for all these things.

Love, Freedom, and Sisterhood

L ast night, I had the great pleasure of going to see Glennon Doyle with my mom in Naples, Florida, at an event called "Love, Freedom and Sisterhood." I've written before about "God winks," and this was a pretty big one. I made plans to take my boys to Florida to see my parents and found out afterwards that Glennon and her new wife, Abby Wambach, would be holding an event only about eight miles from my parents' house while we would be visiting.

For those of you who don't know who Glennon Doyle is, you should look her up. In a nutshell, she is a woman for whom I have a great deal of admiration for several reasons: she speaks her truth, she has learned to find the silver linings in life, and she inspires others to be the best, most honest version of themselves they can be.

After getting sober and writing the blog *Momastery* and the book *Love Warrior,* Glennon focused on philanthropy and activism and started a non-profit called Together Rising. The website says "At Together Rising, we believe that the surest way to lift a family or community is to lift a woman—that when a woman rises, she raises her people up with her. Our mission is our name—To Get Her Rising—and we exist to heal the world, one 'Her' at a time."

I wish everyone could have heard her message last night. There were cameras there filming, so maybe at some point you will be able to see it, but I can at least share some highlights with you:

Become the ones we are waiting for. Through Together Rising, Glennon Doyle has brought immediate help to families that would have otherwise been waiting for long periods of time for aid and assistance. Sometimes, **we** need to be the first responders. I see this firsthand in both my job with the National Breast Center Foundation and as someone in recovery who tries to help and guide others struggling with alcohol or addiction.

The number of women in my own community who don't get the medical treatment they need for breast cancer is staggering. I am blessed to work for an amazing physician who saw this need and started a foundation to address it. Women don't have weeks or months to wait when they are scared, overwhelmed, and lacking insurance or financial resources to get the help and treatment they need. The foundation helps women who need it now.

I also have the privilege of working with many people who turn to me for help with their battle against substance abuse. They may have waited years for help, not knowing where to turn or being too scared to ask. While there are those who disagree with my being so open about my recovery, I think it's fair to say that if I wasn't "out there" with it, I wouldn't have become one of the ones that many are waiting for.

Don't abandon yourself to please the tribe. This was the story of my life until I got sober, worked on my character defects, and stopped being a people-pleaser who was afraid to rock the boat. I spent my life trying to make everyone else happy and worrying about what everyone else thought. I lost myself. I thought for a while that I could find myself in the bottle. Not so much. It only made it worse. Five years and eight months sober (2,070 days, but who's counting), I have only recently started to find out who I really am and speak my truth. Sometimes it's hard as hell, but it's much better than living my life completely numb and abandoning myself to please the tribe.

Get to your own voice of wisdom. Glennon talked about how she often turned to friends for advice and help with major decisions in her life. But she learned that everyone's opinion depends on where they themselves are coming from—their tribe. No one else knows. Only you know. You need to listen to that voice inside of you. Some call it intuition. Some call it wisdom. Glennon described it as "feeling warm." When something doesn't quite feel right, she said she doesn't "feel warm" inside. I think you know what she means. I do. I am blessed to have a few people I trust and confide in, and often run things by to make sure I'm on the right track. But ultimately, I have to listen to my gut. As Glennon said last night, "Your life has never been tried before. Every woman is a pioneer." We will make mistakes in the choices we make in life, but that's okay. The important thing is to learn and grow from them. My mistakes and bad choices made me who I am today. Glennon talked about having our own built-in GPS. It's okay to make a wrong turn and get that voice that says "redirect."

Be still. "Shut out every single voice in your life." We often find our brains on overload with a zillion voices shouting at us, people clamoring for our attention, overwhelmed with life's daily demands. We need to take the time to just be still and tune everything else out. A good friend of mine reminds me often to simply breathe. In recovery, I've learned the importance of prayer and meditation, which comes only with being still. Being still allows me to connect to my Higher Power and refocus. Being still allows me to get to my own voice of wisdom. Being still is also something that is not always easy, especially for someone who is used to going a million miles a minute, but it is essential for us to find our true selves.

Allow nothing but love onto your island. We have the ability to surround ourselves with what we choose. We don't have to allow other people's fear, anger, prejudices, or judgments into our space. Enough said.

Be desperate to tell the truth. When asked about when she started writing her blog, Glennon said that she found it to be something just for her. That she "wrote her heart out." She said that her writing was "raw and real and true, like someone who actually believes she is forgiven." I feel exactly the same way about my writing. There is something amazing about getting it all out and seeing the words on the page. And there is something even more amazing if those words on the page help someone else.

There was so, so much more, but this gives you a good idea. I learned a great deal last night from a fellow recovery warrior, including even a little about carpentry. As Glennon explained, "sistering" means strengthening weak joists with additional material. Adding a board on each side can help a weak one stand stronger. Sometimes, we can all use a little sistering. I've been blessed to have strong women and men stand up beside me to hold me up when I needed it. I hope that I can be a strong board for others when they need it as well.

"If there's a silver lining to the emptiness, here it is: the unfillable is what brings people together. I've never made a friend by bragging about my strengths, but I've made countless by sharing my weakness and my emptiness."
—Glennon Doyle Melton, *Carry On, Warrior: Thoughts on Life Unarmed*

Faith Springs Eternal

Well, spring whirled in with a big snowstorm here in Northern Virginia. Kind of sums up how things have been going for me lately. Haven't had much time to write. For those of you wondering, it's been 2,125 days and I'm still sober. Not something I take for granted, and I am thankful for it every single day. There have been days lately in the chaos that surrounds me when the thought of picking up a drink has crossed my mind. But that's as far as it went. It crossed my mind and then kept on going. But for some, that thought can linger and lead to the actual action of picking up a drink. How do you keep the snowstorm from getting out of control and leading you to pick up that first drink?

Getting sober and staying sober is so often simplified into a few very clear, easy steps: Go to meetings. Don't pick up a drink. Do the next right thing. Help another alcoholic. If the steps are so clear, then why is it so hard? Alcoholism is described as being cunning, baffling, and powerful. All of those are apt descriptions. Cunning is defined as, "Sly, scheming, deceitful, guileful, and foxy." Even "Machiavellian" comes up as a synonym, but that's for another blog piece. The disease is all of those things. It is always lurking, always ready to pounce when your defenses are down. For the newcomer, those defenses may not yet have been developed. But I have heard countless stories of people, sober for years, who let their defenses down and stopped going to meetings, stopped working their recovery program, and ended up picking up a drink again. Then it's off to the races. Because for alcoholics, it's never picking up "a" drink.

Baffling is also a perfect description for the disease because it is so confusing, perplexing, mysterious. It is an obsession of the mind and a physical allergy, malady, or compulsion. There is no magic cure or pill to treat the disease. Alcoholics come in all different shapes and sizes. Alcoholism does not discriminate against age, race, sex, socio-economic background, religion, etc. An alcoholic can go years without a drink and then pick up and be right where he or she left off instantly. Baffling.

And powerful. Well, that is an understatement. When I look at the number of people who relapse and struggle with this disease, I cannot help but appreciate the formidable power of the sickness. It's not until we actually admit that we are powerLESS over the disease and surrender that we can start a path of recovery. Futhermore, we are not strong enough to battle this powerful disease on our own. I've said it before and I will say it again: *We are the only ones who can do it, but we do not have to do it alone.* This is where your HP comes in, or Higher Power. It is said in recovery that "probably no human power could have relieved us of our alcoholism." I know this may be a very controversial statement for many, but I firmly believe that no one can keep you sober—not your sponsor, not your doctor, not your priest, not your spouse, not your best friend. Not even you. It is bigger than you.

A Higher Power is a very personal and individual concept. For some, it is God or spirit. For others, Allah. Some find their Higher Power in nature. Some find it in recovery rooms. One of the things recovery has taught me is to be more open and respectful of the beliefs of others. I believe that willingness, faith, and the ability to turn things over to a power greater than ourselves is essential in recovery. With these things, it is possible to not only keep the cunning, baffling, and powerful foe at bay, but to thrive in a sober, stronger, and better way of life.

I've learned more in the nearly six years I've fought for my sobriety than I have during the rest of my entire life. Some of the most important things being the ones I just mentioned—a willingness to be open and honest, and to work my recovery program. Faith in my Higher Power. And, thanks to my old friend the Serenity Prayer, the ability to differentiate the things that are in and out of my control and knowing when and how to turn things over. For those of you who have seen the cover of my book, *Sobrietease,* you know that the tagline underneath says "Turn It Over." There is an upside-down martini glass, which is, of course, turned over. But the main meaning is turning over the disease to my Higher Power. Surrendering. Asking for help. Putting my ego in the back seat instead of letting it try to run the show.

These things are helpful whether you are in recovery or not. We can all benefit from a willingness to be open and honest. Vulnerability has some extraordinary perks. The Serenity Prayer helps us to keep things in perspective in our daily lives—acceptance of what we cannot change, courage to change what we can, and wisdom to know the difference. And for the things we come to understand we cannot change or are greater than we are, knowing how and when to turn them over to our HP. I've also learned that everyone has their battles and crosses to bear. No matter what that is for you, you are never alone when you rely on your HP.

With those tools, the "simple" steps suggested for getting and staying sober will work and that thought of a drink won't turn into action. Go to meetings. Don't pick up a drink. Do the next right thing. Help another alcoholic. Yes, alcoholism is cunning, baffling, and powerful. But people battle it and win every single day. It can be done. One day at a time. The thought of a drink may come into your mind. Let it keep on going. Whatever you are going through, many things in life will test your willingness and faith. The tests will make you stronger. Doubt will come into your mind often. Let it keep on going. Snowstorms will come...but the snow will melt.

"It is the mark of an educated mind to be able to entertain a thought without accepting it." —Aristotle

Flying Sober

I heard something really powerful today. A fellow alcoholic shared something that was passed along to him: *"Alcohol gave me wings to fly...then it took away the sky."* Just think about that for a few minutes. You may not get that at all. Or it might make perfect sense to you. I completely understand it. I often turned to alcohol for liquid courage. To quell social anxiety when I had to walk into a room full of strangers. To battle depression (it took me years to figure out that trying to fight depression with a depressant wasn't exactly a smart plan). To celebrate and chase a higher high. To escape. To try to stop the pain. To avoid feeling things I didn't want to feel. And when I turned to alcohol for those reasons, I usually did get my wings to fly away from or high above whatever I was avoiding. Or sometimes to fly closer to something I was chasing.

Many people can remember the feeling they got from that very first drink. Most alcoholics will tell you that they instantly knew how much they liked it...a little too much. It may be gradual, but they will continue to try to recreate that buzz, often at great cost. The kid who is shy and quiet might have put a drink or two in him and felt like he was the life of the party. The woman who was afraid to walk into a crowded room full of strangers might have downed a glass of wine, let out a deep breath, and marched in with a new-found confidence. Wings.

Sometimes while we are drinking, we feel invincible. We feel no pain. Hell, I fell down a steep flight of concrete steps and should have been killed, but somehow in my alcoholic stupor, I hobbled away. We feel larger than life. We feel funnier, smarter, stronger, and braver. Wings. Yes, some of those times, maybe we were funny. Maybe we were enjoyable to be around. The life of the party. And then the party ended. But perhaps not for us. As I have said before, I look at my alcoholism as having a broken off-switch. Once I start drinking, there is no telling whether that switch will work or not. While other people may recognize that they have had enough and should probably put on the brakes, I'm only getting warmed up. If I feel good and buzzed, I only want to feel better and fly higher. The off-switch never kicks in.

I am reminded of a Greek myth (hey, I was a Classical Studies major in college, so indulge me here a bit)—the story of Icarus and Daedalus. Daedalus built wings made of branches of osier connected with wax for his son, Icarus, and himself, to escape from the labyrinth in which they were imprisoned on the island of Crete by King Minos. Daedalus warned his son not to fly too high, too close to the sun, or the wax would melt and the wings wouldn't hold up. Icarus was so exhilarated by the thrill of flying that he continued to soar upward. Sure enough, the sun melted the wax, and the boy plummeted into the sea (now known as the Icarian Sea).

Icarus was literally high, but sought to go higher. He paid the price of his life for it. That's what can happen to alcoholics when they get their wings from alcohol. They may think that they soar. Until it takes away their sky. What you think is liquid courage may be "instant asshole" potion. I don't even want to know how obnoxious I truly was when I was lit. Maybe I had the courage to walk into a room full of strangers, but if I continued to drink, chances are I slurred, made little or no sense, embarrassed myself and others, and stumbled out. You seek the light and end up alone in the dark.

Alcohol gave me wings to fly...until I ended up on the cold bathroom floor with my head hanging over the toilet, swearing I would never drink again. Until I did.

Alcohol gave me wings to fly...until my hands were shaking in need of another drink. Alcohol gave me wings to fly... until I lost sight of who I was and what was important in life, and I almost lost all that I cared about. What's ironic is that the higher we try to go, the lower we end up sinking. The closer we get to the sun, the more we get burned. We think we are going toward the light, but we end up in total darkness. Alcohol does, in fact, take away the sky.

The beauty of sobriety is that it is where we find the light. With each day sober, a little brighter ray of light breaks through the cracks. Now, almost six years without a drink, my future is so bright, I gotta wear shades (sorry, I couldn't resist). And, I believe I can fly. Without alcohol. I can fly safely, without crashing. How? By relying on my HP. By reminding myself how much better life is sober than when I was wondering when the wax was going to melt. You too can F.L.Y.—First Love Yourself.

"Until you spread your wings, you'll have no idea how far you can fly." —Napoleon Bonaparte

Wings Optional

I'm a hugger. I like to give and get hugs from people. I understand that some people have personal space issues, but if you're a hugger too, bring it on. I'm also a waver. I grew up in a pretty small town in Western Massachusetts and we waved to each other—as we drove by in cars, rode on our bikes, went for walks, etc. It's such a small, trivial thing, but it makes a difference. People talk about random acts of kindness. We don't have to make grand gestures—start with waving at your neighbor. I drive around or go on my morning walks, and I wave at neighbors and people who pass by. Quite often, they look at me like I have two heads, squint, and try to figure out who I am, and if they don't know they keep on going. Do they really think I'm some sort of friendly, waving, serial killer? Is it that hard to put your hand up, make a gentle wrist motion and acknowledge someone? Thank you to everyone who waves back! And just let me know if you want a hug...

You may have seen the video featuring US Navy Admiral William McRaven who says, "If you want to change the world, start off by making your bed."

Take a minute to watch it on Youtube—it's so worth it. After you make your bed, I add to that, "Wave to your neighbor." I'm not even pushing the hug thing. Admiral McRaven talks about the power of hope. He also says in the speech,

"If you want to change the world, measure a person by the size of their heart, not by the size of their flippers." I haven't been able to measure the size of the hearts of some of the people in my life these days because they are simply too big. These are the people who go way beyond waving and hugging. They give me hope. These are the people who I look at and expect to see wings. They are my angels. I hope that they know who they are. Here are just a few angels I'm sending waves and hugs out to today:

To the woman who summoned up the courage to talk to me through her tears yesterday when I was having coffee and she overheard us talking about the foundation I run that helps women with breast cancer. You're in my prayers.

To the foundation patients I work with who take the time out of their own battles and struggles to send me a note of thanks and tell me that I made a difference in their life. You inspire me.

To the people who reach out with a text or call just to say hi and check on me. And, of course, to the one person who hasn't missed a single day in 2,160 days of sending me my morning ray of sunshine. I'm beyond grateful to you for your unwavering, unconditional love and friendship.

To the man who came up to me at a meeting last week and told me that he read my book...and that it saved his life. Stay strong, my friend.

To the reader in Florida who sent me a tweet to tell me that he was going to be celebrating his first St. Patrick's Day sober and as the designated driver thanks in part to me sharing my journey. Keep going, one day at a time.

To the sweet man in recovery with me who showed up at my door with two guys to fix my broken front door because he knew it was bugging me. He simply said, "I'm your friend. Friends help each other." Yes, they do.

To my brave friend "U.P." who fights a brave fight every day and amazes me with her determination and fortitude. #wegetup

To my friends who donated, shared, re-tweeted, "liked," re-posted, showed up, and helped me surpass our fundraising goal the other night for the foundation. Thank you, each and every one of you. Together we can do great things.

I can't possibly list them all...and I hope those of you I didn't mention know how much I appreciate you, too. Wave to your neighbor and smile at a stranger. You have no idea what is going on in their world. Measure a person by the size of their heart. Little things make a big difference. As Admiral McRaven says, "If you can't do the little things great, you'll never be able to do the big things great."

"You'll meet more angels on a winding path than on a straight one." —Terri Guillemets

A Faded Sparkle
1-800-273-8255
National Suicide
Prevention Lifeline

This morning when I picked up my eyeglasses, I paused for a moment when I saw the Kate Spade name on the frame. The news of her suicide was shocking. A tragic death, leaving behind her husband and 13-year-old daughter. She was a seemingly vibrant, incredibly successful woman in the public eye who clearly suffered privately, battling depression and anxiety. One of the news reports I saw said that she "self-medicated with alcohol." A statement released later by her husband said there was no alcohol or substance abuse. I don't know whether alcohol was one of her demons or not, but it is clear that she had some very powerful ones. I do know that addiction and depression, anxiety and mental illness often go hand-in-hand.

We hear news reports, see posts on social media, and read articles about this fashion icon. But the sad fact is that Kate Spade is now another one of the nearly 45,000 people who die by suicide each year in the United States. Every day, far too many people deal with the devastating loss of a loved one to suicide. Spade's death is a harsh reminder that suicide does not discriminate against age, race, sex, or socio-economic status.

Luckily, there has been an increased focus on suicide prevention in recent days. The novel *13 Reasons Why*, by Jay Asher and released in 2007, was made into a television series in 2017, bringing to light the issue of teen suicide. Just last month, 20 local skateboarders (The DC Wheels) skated 45 miles in pouring rain to fundraise for suicide awareness. And, I'm incredibly proud of my dear childhood friend, Beth Levison, who devoted countless hours over the span of the past several years to produce the award-winning HBO film *32 Pills: My Sister's Suicide*. The movie is about the suicide of a woman named Ruth Litoff and the struggles of her sister, Hope, as she tries to put together the pieces of her sister's demise from mental illness. During the process, Hope succumbs to the devastation and loss, and to her own addiction, and picks up again after 16 years of sobriety. Check it out on Instagram and Facebook at @32pillsmovie.

I am also grateful to have an amazing friend who survived a horrific suicide attempt. It was a long road to recovery, and she still works hard every day to battle her mental illness, but she is not just surviving, she is thriving. She recently reached five years of sobriety, is an extremely talented artist sharing her creative gifts with the world, just got engaged, and has found happiness and love. A true beacon of hope for those who have reached the point of utter desperation to see that things can, in fact, get better. Life is precious and it *can* be beautiful.

Many people are posting the phone number for the **National Suicide Prevention Lifeline (1-800-273-8255)** on their social media pages. Share the number. There is help available. You don't have to suffer alone. Reach out to someone who is hurting. You never know what is going on in someone else's world. The woman you labeled a bitch this morning at Starbucks may be fighting a battle you cannot imagine. Be kind to one another. The website for *32 Pills* has an amazing page of information and resources (http://www.32 Pills Movie.com/Resources). Feel free to share other helpful sites in the comments here or on your own pages. It's a really tough subject, but there is help and hope. Help someone get their sparkle back.

> *"You yourself, as much as anybody in the entire universe, deserve your love and affection."* —Buddha

Dream Weaver

I had a dream last night that I drank a glass of white wine, sitting at a table with friends at some kind of work event. It seemed to be early in the morning, like a breakfast meeting or something. Despite the fact that it was a dream (more like a nightmare for me), I could vividly feel the instantaneous remorse, regret, shame, and guilt. In the dream, I asked the people with me not to tell anyone that I drank the wine, and told them that I didn't want to have to go back and start my count at zero days of sobriety again (as opposed to the 2,265 days that I have accumulated since I stopped drinking six years and two months ago). It was awful.

People in recovery often talk about having "drunk dreams" or "drinking dreams." Some experience them often in their early days of sobriety. Some have them even after decades of not drinking. I woke up so grateful to realize that it was only a dream, but shaken by it enough to write down some thoughts to share. The dream was a good reminder of just how cunning, baffling, and powerful the disease of alcoholism is. It's always ready to pounce. It would be logical to think that most people relapse when things get really difficult in their lives, when tragedy strikes, or when they find themselves in bad shape emotionally, physically, financially, or some other way. But I know people who had gotten sober who simply picked up that drink when all was right in their world. Just because it was a sunny, nice day outside. Just because they thought that they could somehow now "control" their drinking. Or without any forethought, they just poured one and started drinking. In recovery, they say that "we pick up that drink in our minds long before the physical act actually occurs."

For those early in their sober journey, they may just not understand it yet. They may still think that they are able to drink just one beer. Just one glass of wine. If they are alcoholics, they simply cannot. They think this time will be different. That this time they can limit the amount they drink. The true definition of insanity—doing the same thing over and over and expecting a different result. Maybe that one particular time, they will only have one drink. But then there will be the next time. Once the alcohol primes the pump, fuels the disease, triggers that mental obsession and physical compulsion, it's off to the races. And back down to hell.

As we know, the first thing to go out the window when we drink is our judgment. After the first drink, our ability to discern the fact that another drink is not a good plan for us will be dwindling, if not gone already. I have heard countless stories where that idea of just having one drink led down a dark, miserable path of self-destruction and pain. Even death.

Do I really need to be so dramatic about this and use words like hell and death? Yes, I do. Because there are empty chairs in rooms I sit in where people thought that one drink wouldn't hurt them. Because I have seen first-hand the path of wreckage and destruction left behind by someone who made that choice to pick up the first drink, again. And because the cunning, baffling, powerful disease from which I suffer has tried to tell me that I, too, can maybe just have one drink now. That maybe six years is long enough and I have somehow (miraculously) garnered the power and mystical ability to control my drinking. It can tempt me by a dream that has me drink a glass of wine and seem fine. But even in that dream, my gut told me it was wrong. We tell our kids to listen to their guts to help them discern right from wrong. If you get that bad feeling inside, you know you're not on the right path. How amazing that even in our dream state, we can get that feeling in our gut. As I said previously, I could vividly feel immediate remorse and regret after I drank the wine in the dream. And shame. Enough shame to ask the people around me to keep the fact that I drank a glass of wine a secret. We are only as sick as our secrets. Clearly, this alcoholic still has a great deal of work to do.

I've been told that these dreams will happen. Cravings will still come. Whether you have six days, six years, or six decades of sobriety, you have to always stay vigilant. Do not let that drink devil that sits on your shoulder and whispers nonsense in your ear win. Do not get complacent. The disease of alcoholism will continue to do pushups every day. Be stronger. Dream bigger. Dream brighter. I'm on to day 2,266 tomorrow—take that, Dream Weaver.

> *"I have had dreams and I have had nightmares, but I conquered my nightmares because of my dreams."*
> —Jonas Salk

Life on Life's Terms

Today marks 2,300 days of sobriety. Not sure if there is any particular significance to that number, other than it's 2,300 days without picking up a drink. Two thousand three hundred days of not succumbing to temptations or cravings. Two thousand three hundred days of learning that life is so much better sober. Two thousand three hundred days of not choosing numbness over feelings, even if those feelings are painful. Two thousand three hundred days of not relying on alcohol to provide me with an escape from reality. Two thousand three hundred days of no hangovers. Two thousand three hundred days of being present. Two thousand three hundred days, one day at a time. Two thousand three hundred days stronger. Basically, 2,300 days of living life on life's terms.

Please don't get me wrong—while I can honestly say that life is so much better sober, it does not mean that life is by any means easy or all rainbows and sunshine. Bad things happen in life, whether we are sober or inebriated. I used to do a great job of convincing myself that it was easier to deal with difficult times by escaping reality and anesthetizing myself with alcohol. If I simply ignored the things I didn't want to deal with, perhaps they would go away. Funny, that never seemed to work. They would still be there in the morning, along with a miserable hangover and pounding headache.

Yes, life is tough. But what I wish I could convey to people who are still struggling with addiction and alcoholism, still smothered with hopelessness and despair, is that the difference when you get to the other side boils down to one simple thing: *hope*. Miraculously, recovery has given me the incredible peace of mind and comfort that somehow, someway, everything will turn out okay. As. Long. As. I. Don't. Pick. Up. A. Drink. Or, put another way, as a friend in recovery often says, "Not even if your ass is on fire."

I've been dealing with significant health issues for over 14 months now. To say that I've been frustrated is a huge understatement. For a person who is used to going full-speed (and then some) to not have the energy or stamina to make it half-way through the day has been brutal. Being in a constant state of pain and exhaustion has taken its toll, not only on me, but on those closest to me I'm sure. As days of feeling crappy turned into weeks, and then into months and a year, I won't lie and tell you that I didn't think about picking up a drink. I did. Several times. But I remembered: Not even if my ass is on fire. Two thousand three hundred days of sobriety has taught me that no matter what, a drink would only make things worse. Much worse.

I'm finally starting to see a light at the end of the tunnel. I've written many pieces about the trying to find the silver lining in all situations, something that a very dear friend has taught me. While this whole ordeal has been pretty damn miserable, I have been able to take away a few key lessons. First and foremost, I have learned to put myself first. I do that with my sobriety, because if I don't have my sobriety, I won't have anything else. But physical and emotional health go hand-in-hand with that. I've learned to listen to my body and that when I'm exhausted, I need to rest. And that it's okay to rest. Without feeling guilty. For many of us, especially moms, it's been drilled into us by society that we have to go a million miles an hour, take care of everyone and everything, and be constantly on the move, doing something productive at all times. We often put ourselves last on our lists, if we even make it on there at all. Self-care is not a luxury. It is imperative.

I've also learned to prioritize and reassess what is truly important. It shouldn't take being sick to do this, but it is what it is. When you have limited energy and capacity, you have to be realistic about what you actually can do and what really needs to be done. And what can take a backseat. It's often probably more than you might think.

I also came to understand that it's okay to wave the white flag and ask for help. Since my sobriety is very much at the top of that list of priorities and what is truly important, and sometimes getting to meetings isn't an option because I'm not feeling well enough to attend, I reach out to friends in recovery and they graciously bring a meeting to me. Or, if my tank is running on fumes, I choose a meeting over doing a load of laundry. Filling up my tank with fuel for staying sober is more important than loading up the washing machine dispenser with Tide. Clean living over clean laundry. Sorry, I'm getting carried away...

Self-care is crucial for everyone, not just those in recovery. Taking care of yourself, in every way that is important, will allow you to live life on life's terms. On the good days and on the bad days. On the days when it feels like your ass is on fire. Be kind to yourself. Put yourself first on your list. Aim for more days of rainbows and sunshine and you just might get there.

"An empty lantern provides no light. Self-care is the fuel that allows your light to shine brightly." —Unknown

Menace to Sobriety

I just wrapped up a huge work event that has consumed my time over the last several months. Between that and coming off the heels of being very sick for over a year, I haven't written much. Feels good to start typing.

The work event was the Third Annual Walk to Bust Cancer, which benefits the National Breast Center Foundation, of which I am the Executive Director. This year's walk drew over 700 people and far surpassed our fundraising goal of $75,000. I was incredibly blessed to work with an amazing team of volunteers on this event; most of them breast cancer survivors who just want to give back. The walk is a giant undertaking, with an inordinate amount of logistics, man-hours, details and, yes, stress.

Being sick for over 14 months, without answers or a diagnosis, also created a great deal of stress. Endless trips to doctors, hospitals, specialists, labs, etc. with no concrete results. Finally, two different doctors came to the same conclusion: fibromyalgia. An answer, but one with a great deal of mystery and uncertainty surrounding it. While much is still unknown about the disorder, and the extremely long amount of time it took to diagnose, it left me beyond frustrated, I am relieved and grateful that the medicine that they put me on to treat it is helping immensely. Interestingly enough, one of the worst things and triggers for fibromyalgia? Stress.

We all have stress in our lives. At some times, greater amounts than others. And some people are better at dealing with stress than others. There are those who go to yoga and meditate and are able to successfully keep their stress at bay. Others work out intensely and release endorphins to combat the pressure, anxiety, and tension in their lives. And many others still who pour that glass of wine or scotch or whatever to take the edge off. I was one of those. So, what does one do to combat stress when he or she can no longer reach for the numbing effects of alcohol?

Two thousand three hundred thirty-six days ago, when I accepted and admitted the fact that I was an alcoholic, I made a firm commitment to never reach for that glass of wine again. Well, not "never," just one day at a time. But whether it was to celebrate something or to drown my sorrows, or yes, to battle whatever stress factors were attacking me at the time, I knew that booze could no longer be my go-to. Not unless I wanted to continue the downward spiral and destructive path that my disease had me on.

There will inevitably be periods of stress in our lives. I mentioned some healthy ways to deal with them: yoga, exercise, meditation. But how do we remember to do those things when we are so stressed out? Or how do we make time for them when time constraints add to our stress in the first place?? Now that I am sober, it's so clear to me how awful drinking was for trying to combat stress. While it provided a very temporary reprieve, when I threw caution to the wind and simply enjoyed the buzz, the resulting hangover and usual aftermath almost always somehow increased my stress level.

I often spent the morning trying to piece together what I had done the night before, sometimes having no recollection whatsoever. I missed appointments, commitments, or meetings because I was too hungover to keep them. I often had to lie, either to cover up idiotic, drunken decisions or behavior, or to try to hide how much I was suffering from the effects of my drinking. Many times, I would act extra chipper on those mornings when my head was pounding and I was fighting the feeling of having to throw up. I didn't want my husband, children, or work colleagues to know how badly I was hurting. Does lying contribute to stress? I'll let you answer that.

Fast forward to today. During the long period of feeling like absolute crap this past year, now explained by my fibromyalgia diagnosis, many people commented to me about how amazed they were that I managed to stay so positive and keep a smile on my face (definitely not always, but I tried). I relished in the miracle that throughout all the anger, frustration, exhaustion, illness, and disappointment, I had learned, and I knew, that a drink would not make it the least bit better. In fact, I finally understood that it would have just the opposite effect. Because it wouldn't be just "a" drink. It would be many. Once I opened that can of worms, it would be all downhill from there. All the hard work, out the window.

So I am slowly making my way back to yoga, which helped me immensely when I first got sober almost six and a half years ago. I'm better at listening to my body and taking it easy when I have to. I have also incorporated a daily meditation practice into my routine, which has made a huge difference in how I handle and manage stress. Frankly, a huge difference in how I handle life in general. I'm very grateful to a dear friend who encouraged this and walks the walk beautifully. I'm also gradually getting back to the gym and trying to exercise. All of which will be huge factors in combating my fibromyalgia.

But my one consistent fallback and most powerful weapon against stress is the Serenity Prayer. Is it something I can control or do something about? If it isn't, I remind myself to let it go. To turn it over. And it never hurts to have that simple, powerful reminder: breathe.

"Breathe. Let go. And remind yourself that this very moment is the only one you know you have for sure."
—Oprah Winfrey

Selfish?

I must have heard it hundreds of times as my children were growing up. Someone would see them in the stroller or in my arms and comment on how fast the time goes and how quickly they grow. They spoke from experience, longingly remembering the days when their own children were small enough to ride in a stroller or be carried. They were right. The time goes so quickly. As I help my oldest child with college applications, getting ready to send her off next year, I can't help think that those days of diapers and bottles were just yesterday.

I'm writing this piece, as I usually do, to share my story with others in the hope of helping someone who is struggling. But today, I'm also writing this as a reminder to myself. On the days when the intense battle to resist the urge of picking up a drink ramps up, it's helpful to be reminded of the joys of sobriety. The gift of being present is way up there. I've heard so many heartbreaking stories about families torn apart by alcoholism and addiction. People who are estranged from their children or parents. Older generations not allowed to spend time with their own grandchildren. Friends cut off completely by loved ones because of their repeated offenses while drinking or using. I have had it clearly presented to me exactly what could have happened had I continued down the path I was on.

But today, as I read my daughter's college essay, I am filled with gratitude and appreciation for the gift of sobriety. And for the opportunity to understand what that means to her. While the first line of her essay might suggest otherwise, my daughter has benefitted from my recovery more than I might have thought. She begins her essay by saying, "My mom is selfish." Yup. I am. My sobriety comes first and foremost, and for that I will not apologize, even to friends and people in my life who don't understand and criticize me for that. My daughter goes on to say that she has learned that it is not only okay to put ourselves first, it is essential and actually selfless, in order to be the best version of ourselves that we can be and to help those around us. I had shared with her my analogy of oxygen masks on an airplane. Parents are always told that they should secure their own masks first so that they can then be able to assist their children with theirs. My daughter describes how she has come to understand that I had to secure my own sobriety first so that I could assist her (and her brothers) in keeping safe on the airplane, or that crazy roller coaster called life.

She also questions her own role and responsibility in my recovery. I am also grateful to read that she understands that ultimately, no one else can stop me from picking up that first drink. That's all me. Not her. Not anyone. The choice is mine. And I have to do the work and all that I can to not let that happen. But those who love me, like she does, can be there to support, encourage, and ensure that my oxygen mask is still secured. To tighten it when it gets too loose. To remind me to put it back on if I get too cocky or complacent.

Her first choice for school next year is my alma mater. In a corny act of superstition/hope for good luck/acceptance "rain dance," I put on my college sweatshirt, torn and tattered from so many years of wear, and we pushed the send button together on the computer and submitted her application. Now we wait. I have told her that it's out of our hands. That she will end up at the best place for her, even if it isn't her first choice. I remember well what a stressful time it was for me, and I am grateful that I am sober and present to ride through this part of the roller coaster with her. And when the ride gets really bumpy, I'll make sure my mask is on securely and double-check hers. I am selfish. So is she. And I'm so proud of her.

> *"It is not selfish to love yourself, take care of yourself, and to make your happiness a priority. It's necessary."* —Mandy Hale

#wegetup

The motto on the back of this year's survivor t-shirts at the Walk to Bust Cancer a few weeks ago was "#wegetup." It's the motto of a dear friend of mine, who inspires me and so many others with her unfaltering determination and positive attitude throughout her ongoing battle. When she found out that her breast cancer had metastasized to her brain, she signed off on all her texts, emails, and posts with "#wegetup." A reminder to herself and others that we will all get knocked down in life, but we have to get back up. Many times, that is a very tall order.

#wegetup is the motto of the U.S. Figure Skating Association. When the campaign was launched in 2016, U.S. Figure Skating Association chief marketing officer, Ramsey Baker, said, "We all fall, it's how we get up that matters." My brave friend Mary reached out to the USFSA and explained why the motto was so important to her and received permission for us to use it for our local breast cancer walk. It was pretty amazing to look out at the crowd and see so many bright pink shirts proudly worn by survivors, those who had been knocked down but got up to fight, walk, support, and encourage others to do the same.

Throughout my journey of sobriety, I've known many people who have fallen/slipped/relapsed or "gone out to do more research," as we like to say in recovery. Unfortunately, some of them never made it back in. But so many pull themselves back up, brush themselves off, throw away the bottles or pour the rest down the sink, and start at day one again. At step one. Sometimes several times. Progress, not perfection.

I remember asking a close friend early in my sobriety what she would do if I drank again. She said it would depend on if and how I get back up. I've made it almost six and a half years now, but that doesn't mean for one second that I am out of the woods. I never will be. I can never take my sobriety for granted, get cocky or complacent, or think that somehow, I have this cunning, baffling, and powerful disease beat. When I hear of people who have been sober for decades slipping, it reinforces my vigilance.

I used to figure skate as a child. That ice is cold when you fall. And it's hard and it hurts. The longer you stay down, the colder you get and the more it hurts. Same with drinking. Add darker to that mix. A darker, colder, harder, and deadlier spiral down. There's nothing wrong with asking for a hand to pull you back up. #wegetup—but we don't have to do it alone.

We all get knocked down at some point. By something or someone. Everyone has their struggles. If you are lucky enough to have had a hand reach down and pull you back up, be grateful. If you pulled yourself up by your own bootstraps, be proud. If you were down for longer than you had hoped, be gentle on yourself. If you're still down, ask for help. Remember the brave warriors who have gone before you who told themselves that #wegetup...and did.

"Sometimes you have to get knocked down lower than you have ever been, to stand up taller than you ever were." —Anonymous

Turn the Page

A new year brings with it the opportunity to turn to a blank page in a brand new book, full of possibilities for you to write your own story going forward. Like many, I find myself introspective at the end of each year, looking back at the highs and lows, and peering forward optimistically at what might come. I had grandiose ideas of writing a long piece exploring all of those things in greater detail, but, again, like many, I find myself out of steam as the year comes to a close.

This piece will be brief. A simple thank you to those of you who have followed my blog this year. Thank you for the kind words from people who have shared that my book or blog helped them get through a rough time, stay sober, or change their perspective on life for the better.

I'll close out 2018 with 2,409 days of sobriety under my belt. Not something I take lightly. There were many days when it looked like I might be starting back at day one again. But I pushed through. And for that, I am grateful to those of you who stood by me, lent a helping hand or shoulder, reminded me that I am strong and how hard I fought to get where I am today. Most importantly, thank you for the reminder that I am not alone in this journey.

As for resolutions, I have thought of many, but I'm leaving you with two quotes for the new year from people much smarter than I am:

"Always bear in mind that your own resolution to succeed is more important than any other."
—Abraham Lincoln

"Ring out the false, ring in the true."
—Alfred Lord Tennyson

Happy New Year.

Present Emotions Included

Most of the books piled up on the side of my bed fall under the category of self-help. There are so many amazing ones out there. I could fill an entire book just sharing what I learned from some of them. I've referred to the idea that I call "recycling the light" in previous blogs that I have written. I try to pass along things that I've read, heard, or learned that might help others. I almost always include an inspirational quote with my pieces because there are millions of wise people who have said things so much more eloquently than I ever possibly could. A great deal of what I read focuses on being positive and living your life as your authentic self. Wonderful concepts in theory, but often much easier said than done.

Books like *The Power of Positive Thinking* by Norman Vincent Peale, *Change Your Thoughts, Change Your Life* and *The Power of Intention* by Dr. Wayne Dyer, and *The Law of Attraction* and *Ask and It Is Given* by Jerry and Esther Hicks helped me understand that we can change our lives for the better by simply focusing on the positive and raising our vibrational level to attract what we desire. *The Secret* by Rhonda Byrne took the world by storm a decade ago with the concept that by simply envisioning and believing that we will receive what we want will result in it ultimately manifesting itself. I could go on...but like I said, great in theory, but difficult to always stick to. How do you stay positive and believe when life gets really tough? Should I just sing the song "Don't Worry, Be Happy" by Bobby McFerrin and pretend all is well?

A woman who I greatly admire and am honored to call a friend, Maimah Karmo, recently said, "More so than my successes, it was the times of struggle that showed me what I was made of." I had the pleasure of participating in Maimah's "I Manifest Online Soul Summit" and doing a podcast with her called "How to Overcome Hurt by Being Present in Your Life." As an alcoholic, I was anything but "present" for so much of my life. I used alcohol to escape reality or numb feelings I didn't want to feel. So, "overcoming hurt by being present?" Yes. Face your demons head-on. Use your tools to resist the urge to escape, numb, or run away from reality. Stay in the moment instead of beating yourself up and dwelling on the past or constantly investing in the wreckage of the future.

But back to Maimah's quote. It's easier to stay positive and be present when things are going well and we can celebrate our successes. Times of struggle show us what we are truly made of. It's when the shit hits the fan that we are really tested. When faced with difficult challenges, Bobby McFerrin's isn't the first song that pops into the song chart in my head. Maybe a little something heavier, like Depeche Mode's "Blasphemous Rumors" perhaps. Oh, no wait—The Smiths. Morrissey is always great for wallowing in self-pity. I digress. My point is this: Bad things will happen in life, whether you are sober or not. It's how you deal with them and how you move on that shows what you are made of.

Not only are there zillions of self-help books out there, there is an entire movement happening that is bringing people to meditation, living in the present moment, and understanding our universal connectedness. Some of the most popular downloaded apps these days are for mindfulness and meditation. There are countless workshops, retreats, seminars, webinars, conferences, etc. that focus on spirituality, emotional and physical health, and overall mind-body wellness. I had the pleasure of attending an event last week at a local concert hall which has attracted some of the biggest names in the music business over the years. But instead of music, the featured act was a man named Kyle Cease—a former stand-up comedian, now a transformational speaker who incorporates his humor and personal evolution for an incredibly entertaining and inspirational evening. Kyle emphasizes that "when you embrace your pain, fear, and vulnerability instead of pushing it away, you will discover an authentic creativity and power that is truly unstoppable."

Embracing your feelings when you are being present is not easy, especially when that feeling is fear or pain. But if we can somehow train ourselves to sit with being uncomfortable, embrace it and then LET IT GO, we can move on. Life will have ups and downs. As hard as the downs can be, I truly believe that it is better to be present for them rather than numb or escape them. Experiencing the downs, although incredibly difficult at times, allows us to not only truly appreciate and treasure the ups, but hopefully learn something and take away a lesson that will help us in the future and ultimately make us stronger. I'm always grateful to my dear friend who teaches me to find the silver lining in all situations. Things could always be better, but they can always be worse too. All we truly have is the present. Don't get caught up in the past or waste time worrying about the future, which is never guaranteed. Breathe. Smile. And live.

"It's not 'When something happens, I'll be happy.' It's 'When I'm happy, things will happen.'"
—Kyle Cease, *Evolving Out Loud*

Sober Doesn't Have to Be Somber

I remember when I first stopped drinking, almost seven years ago, I couldn't fathom that I would never be able to pick up a drink again. How would life ever be fun without my personality lube? How would I socialize without my liquid courage? Would everyone see me as boring as they knocked 'em back and I sat quietly and drank my seltzer? I really couldn't imagine the change I needed to make. I only knew that I had to make it, or I would continue heading down a deadly path.

There is a saying in recovery: "Change I must or die I will." It's not enough to just stop drinking. We must change who we are at the core. We must examine the things that made us want to escape into the bottle. Look at our character defects and face them head-on. Figure out what people, places, and things served as triggers for our drinking and avoid them like the plague. Dissect our resentments and fears and conquer them. It is an all-out revamping, remodeling, rebuilding, and recreating who we were. Stronger, healthier, wiser, and more at peace and comfortable in our own skin. Do you remember the show *The Six Million Dollar Man*? Steve Austin? "Gentlemen. We can rebuild him. We have the technology. Better than he was before. Better.

Stronger. Faster." Okay, well maybe sobriety won't get you all those things. But definitely better.

We get the "technology" or tools we need during recovery to rebuild ourselves better than before. It's far from easy. It takes time and a great deal of effort. Often lots of blood, sweat, and tears. And, as I've said many times over, we're the only ones who can do it, but we don't have to do it alone. We can pick up a drink...or we can pick up the phone. We can pour something that will eventually kill us over ice or we can pore over the pages of literature written by those who are much wiser and have gone before us, sharing their experience, strength, and hope.

But does all of this make us boring and no fun to be around? What if we used to be the life of the party when we drank? Or maybe we just thought we were the life of the party? In either case, if we were used to our social lives revolving around alcohol—parties, bars, concerts, etc.—how do we make that change to a sober life without it being somber? And dull.

I'm going to be perfectly honest. Early in my sobriety it was beyond somber. It was miserable. Dark. Gray. Depressing. Scary. Lonely. I felt like I had lost my best friend. I mourned the breakup by staying in bed, getting over the physical symptoms of detoxing, for months. When I physically started to feel better, I faced the cold hard truth that I could no longer put myself in situations where people, places, and things would trigger me to want to pick up a drink. Since drinking was pretty much all I knew, that was basically everyone, everywhere, and everything. So I stayed in my bed even longer.

As I got myself into a recovery program, I learned that isolating was not a good idea. I had to force myself to get out of my own head and be with other people. I was blessed with some amazing friends who wouldn't let me stay in my bed forever, despite my best efforts. They got me to join an exercise program, a Bible study, or go for walks. I found other recovering alcoholics who would text me, especially on Friday nights at 5 p.m. when that dreaded happy hour rolled around. They knew how much I was struggling and trying to adjust to fill that time with something else besides my usual glass (OK, bottles) of wine.

Eventually, I managed to go to a few social outings. I didn't last long and always had an "escape plan." But I gradually got some strength to figure out how to still have a life while not drinking. I'll never forget going to a neighborhood pool party with a dear friend who tried to pull me out to dance. I told her that I couldn't dance sober. She reminded me that I couldn't actually dance drunk either. We both got a great laugh out of it. And yes, I did dance. And I had fun.

Little by little, as each day went by, I got stronger and could do more socializing. I could go to restaurants and not drool every time a waiter walked by with a tray of martinis heading to another table. I could go to a friend's house and see people drinking wine while I had seltzer and not want to scream that life was unfair. I could see someone holding a red Solo cup at our neighborhood pool and not obsess about what was in it, knowing full well it was an alcoholic beverage. I've shared before that we even hosted "Mocktail Parties," where people created their own fun, non-alcoholic beverages and competed for the best tasting and best named drinks. My kids even joined in this party, making their own concoctions and socializing with a bunch of sober adults.

I even started going on trips to see friends and learned to travel without drinking. Instead of researching which restaurants had the best wine lists or bars, I looked for other things in advance of my trips. Places to hike, spas, and recovery meetings I could attend. And guess what? I had fun. I remembered where I went, what I did and who I met. I didn't wake up with a massive hangover and was able to enjoy the day. And the night. And the company I was with. All while knowing I didn't make any more of an ass of myself than I would sober.

I recently went to Colorado to see a dear friend who was with me when I had my last drink and was the first person I told that I was an alcoholic. We actually sat at the bar at the base of the mountain and had something to eat and a (nonalcoholic) drink at the end of a day of skiing. We talked about how far I had come to be able to sit at a bar, facing bottles of alcohol, and not be totally freaked out.

So for those of you who may be early in your sobriety and struggling, wondering if life will ever be fun without the booze, I can tell you honestly that it will. It will be so much better. In so many ways. Call me crazy, but what I used to think was fun often came with me spending a lot of time on the cold bathroom floor holding on to the toilet, vowing to never drink again. Or with my head pounding so hard that I had to shush my kids every time they spoke. Or cancelling all my plans to simply nurse my hangover in bed. Or straining my brain (what was left after all the brain cells I had killed) to figure out what I had done the night before that I might be embarrassed about.

I may not be dancing on tables (and based on my friend's comment, I'd say that is a good thing), but I am far from somber. Sobriety has given me many gifts, including a life that is happy, joyous, and free. And the gratitude and clarity to appreciate all that comes with sobriety. Somber is defined as "dark or dull in color or tone; gloomy." Sobriety has brought back the rainbows in my life.

"No really, you're an excellent dancer." —Jose Cuervo, Robert Mondavi, Jack Daniels, Jim Beam...

A Sip Not a Slip

I had absolutely no intention of putting a glass of vodka mixed with cranberry juice to my mouth. No desire to have it touch my lips and wash against my tongue. In fact, when it did, my reaction was so strong, it surprised me. I immediately recognized that it was not my drink (cranberry juice and club soda), and once I realized that there was a strong amount of alcohol in the drink that I picked up, I turned away from the two women standing next to me and spit it out. And spit again. And again. I think wiped my tongue with my sleeve. And then wiped my lips. Repeatedly. I have not had a drink that contained alcohol in nearly seven years (2,537 days to be exact). What used to be so familiar to me was now a very, very unwelcome stranger.

I'm pretty sure I simply said, "Well, that was not my drink!" The woman whose drink I accidentally picked up apologized profusely. She knew I didn't drink. Totally not her fault. The drinks looked identical. Both had lime garnishes. Both a pinkish-red hue from the cranberry juice. But one had an ingredient that was clearly not okay for an alcoholic. I walked away to return to the work event I was attending. The other woman, a good friend of mine, came over to me and asked if I was okay. I told her that I was more than a little freaked out at having picked up an alcoholic drink. She told me not to be too hard on myself, not to give it a second thought, since I clearly hadn't done it on purpose. I let it go...for the time being.

When I got in my car, I picked up my phone to call a friend who is also in recovery. But then I hesitated. For a few seconds, I worried that if I told her what had happened, she would tell me I should reset my start date and begin again at day one. I thought about not telling her. I think that scared me more than picking up the drink. Sobriety requires "rigorous honesty." Keeping a secret about something that clearly bothered me, considerably, was not a good plan. It doesn't matter that other people may think it was totally innocent, no big deal, that I was overreacting, whatever. The fact was that I was more than a little flustered about tasting vodka again, even for a split second. I dialed the number and told her what happened. She told me it had happened to her, several times, that it was okay, clearly not intentional, that I didn't fake it and swallow it and continue to drink the wrong drink, and that I did the right thing. She said it was a "sip, not a slip." I felt much better.

As Elvis Costello will tell you, accidents will happen. Chances are good that something like that will happen again. I'm actually quite glad that my reaction was so strong. That I didn't taste the vodka and feel like I missed it and wanted more. I'm grateful that I woke up today with another day of sobriety under my belt. Grateful to wake up without a hangover. Grateful it was a sip, not a slip.

"There are no accidents...there is only some purpose that we haven't yet understood." —Ritu Ghatourey

Squirrelly About Seven

It usually happens to some extent every year. A little before the anniversary of my sobriety date, I get squirrelly. I get anxious. Restless, irritable, and discontent. Excited, but scared. Proud, but cautious. This year seems worse than previous ones. Maybe it's the number seven. Seven seas. Seven continents. Seven days of the week. Seven colors of the rainbow. Seven years of sobriety, God-willing, on May 28. Many people would say I shouldn't even write that and risk jinxing myself. But I do. Because it's an important date. It's the day my life changed for the better.

So why squirrelly? Why anxious? Do I want to pick up a drink? No. Have I thought about it? Many times. It's a bittersweet weekend for me. Memorial Day weekend in 2012 was the last time I drank. And I drank a lot. And then some. My hands shook at 11 a.m. until I got some wine in me. The weekend ended with me admitting that I was powerless over alcohol. That my life had become unmanageable. I made the decision to get help, and it was the best thing I have ever done. It was hard as hell, but 2,553 days later, I have not had a drink. I had that scare I wrote about in my last post ("A Sip Not a Slip"), when I accidentally picked up a drink with vodka in it, but I have not intentionally picked up a drink in a long, long time.

From what I have learned over these past nearly seven years, my squirrely feelings are quite common among people in recovery. There's something about facing the anniversary of the last drink that brings up a lot. I look at the weekend ahead, which will be filled with those #^%@#& red Solo cups at pools, backyard barbeques, parties, etc. Coolers filled with cold beer. Wine glasses with beads of sweat dripping down the side. And more. And then I think about making it through the weekend to Tuesday. And about reaching another milestone in this personal battle. I think about how much better my life is without the booze. Without the hangovers. Without the blackouts. Without the poison that took its toll on my body.

Don't get me wrong...life isn't all sunshine and rainbows just because I don't drink. The shitstorms still come, and if you looked at the Doppler radar in my life right now, you'd see a huge storm raging right above me that hasn't been clearing for quite some time. But, as I've heard repeatedly, there's no problem that picking up a drink won't make worse. Jose Cuervo has no power over the storm clouds. But my Higher Power does. Sometimes I write what I need to read, hear, and remind myself.

"Hope begins in the dark, the stubborn hope that if you just show up and try and do the right thing, the dawn will come. You wait and watch and work: you don't give up." —Anne Lamott

A Toast to the Graduates

When I first got sober, I used to worry about how I would deal with a champagne toast at my daughter's wedding. Of course, that will be years from now, but hey, why not worry about things now right? What I didn't think about was toasting other major occasions, like her high school graduation, which was this past week. And I almost got through it without having to think about it at all. Almost.

It was a beautiful ceremony. I was so happy to be there with my whole family, including my parents. My daughter graduated summa cum laude and I was so proud of her. I beamed as I watched her cross the stage to receive her diploma in her cap and gown and hood in bright school colors. For a few seconds, I thought about the fact that if I were still drinking, I'd probably be miserably hungover for this milestone in her life. Either that, or I'd be just plain drunk.

The thought of drinking to celebrate her graduation now had never even occurred to me. We went out for a celebratory lunch immediately after graduation. Water and a cappuccino suited me just fine. At the end of lunch, as desserts came out, the manager of the restaurant approached our table with a bottle of champagne in one hand and several glasses held between the fingers of the other. It was a lovely gesture. He put the glass in front of me and then the other adults at the table. He spoke to my father a bit as he worked to loosen the cork from the bottle. As it finally gave way with a loud pop, he approached my seat to pour the light gold liquid into my glass. It was easier than I had ever antici-pated to simply say, "Thank you, but I'm not having any."

The world didn't come to an end. Everyone didn't freeze mid-sentence and stare at me in an awkward silence. The manager didn't drop his jaw in shock at the fact that I had refused his kind offering. No, no one really cared that I turned down a glass of champagne. Most importantly, I didn't care. I didn't miss it. I didn't pout. I enjoyed being present and able to celebrate a special day knowing I would remember it in the future and wake up without a hangover.

My son graduates from elementary school next week. Sparkling cider all around.

Congratulations to all the graduates out there, especially two very dear to me.

"The more you praise and celebrate your life, the more there is in life to celebrate." —Oprah Winfrey

Apprehended by Grace

Many people ask me what my rock bottom was. What finally made me stop drinking. When I admitted the fact that I was an alcoholic and surrendered. I can give you a long list of when it SHOULD have been. When friendships were torn apart. When my marriage started suffering. When my mother and close friends expressed their concerns about how much I was drinking. When I looked in the mirror and saw how bloated and puffy my face was and how red my eyes were. When I started having health problems. When I was doing even more idiotic, embarrassing, and shameful things than usual. When I fell down a steep set of stairs, completely intoxicated, and should have been killed. When I continuously woke up not remembering what I had done or said the night before. Nope. None of those things did it.

Everyone's rock bottom is different. I know many people in recovery who spent time in jail, received DWIs, crashed cars, lost jobs, homes, families and friends, lived on the streets or in their cars, and had much lower rock bottoms than I did. Others, like me, had what may be considered "high bottoms," but they are just as much alcoholics as the others. I once heard someone say that it's not how much you drink but how the drinking affects you that matters. Just as there are different rock bottoms, there are different types of alcoholics. Binge drinkers. Daily drinkers. Maintenance drinkers. Bar drinkers. Isolation drinkers. Social drinkers. Heck, I even went to college with a girl named Margarita Drinker. No lie. Her parents had quite a sense of humor, I guess. Or named her after having a bit too much tequila themselves. But I digress...

The point is that there is no singular description of the alcoholic. No scale that tells you once you fall below a certain level, you have hit your rock bottom. It is different for everyone. But at some moment, at some point, many people are somehow, and perhaps miraculously, *apprehended by grace.* I believe that is the moment when people finally surrender. It may be in utter despair. It may be when you realize you are simply sick and tired of being sick and tired. It may be while looking in the mirror and not able to face the person looking back at you any longer. It may be after fighting back and resisting, be it an intervention, attending a recovery program as a "guest of the judge," while at rehab or in the pscyh ward, or while dishing out your last dollar at the liquor store. However it comes, it is when you finally realize and accept that you cannot continue to live your life like this. That you cannot fight this battle alone. That only a power greater than yourself can restore you to sanity. It is when you wave the white flag and surrender to your Higher Power, whatever that may be for you, and at that moment, I believe that you are *apprehended by grace.*

For me, my surrender came seven years ago in NYC. I've shared the story many times. My hands were shaking until I got a drink in me at 11 a.m. I was a mess, physically and emotionally. Looked and felt horrible. I had known for so long that I could not continue drinking the way I had been, but I could not imagine my life without alcohol. It dominated

134

every aspect of my life. Hell, it was my life. It was both my best friend and my worst enemy. How do you fight your worst enemy and get rid of them while losing your best friend at the same time? But as I sat there with my *true* best friend who lost her husband to alcoholism, I was, in fact, miraculously apprehended by grace, and I was finally able to admit that I had a drinking problem. It was as if a 3,000-pound weight was lifted from my shoulders.

I believe that being apprehended by grace goes hand in hand with receiving the gift of humility. To accept and realize that we are only human, that we cannot fix everything, including ourselves, and come to understand that our Higher Power can, is a true blessing. We somehow grasp that not only can we turn things over, we must. One of the definitions of grace is the "free and unmerited favor of God." Free. Unmerited. We don't need to do anything to earn it or receive it. We simply need to be willing to ask. And surrender. To allow ourselves to be apprehended by grace.

Because we are human, we can forget. We can stray. We can try to escape after having been apprehended. Foolishly. But yet we still do it. Staying on the right track, whatever that looks like for you, can keep you living a life of grace. It may be prayer, meditation, working a recovery program, or however you continuously remind yourself to rely on and turn to your Higher Power.

I am so incredibly grateful to have been apprehended by grace. To have found the path to a better life. Free from the bondage of addiction. It doesn't come easy many days, but if I remember to practice what I preach, to turn things over to my Higher Power and stay humble, it gets easier to find my way back to the right path.

"For grace is given not because we have done good works, but in order that we may be able to do them."
—Saint Augustine of Hippo

"Grace comes into the soul, as the morning sun into the world; first a dawning, then a light; and at last the sun in his full and excellent brightness."
—Thomas Adams

"The meaning of life. The wasted years of life. The poor choices of life. God answers the mess of life with one word: 'Grace.'" —Max Lucado

Trigger Happy

After being sober for seven years now, I've learned how to deal with several of the triggers that bring out my urge to drink. It took several years before I was able to comfortably go to social events and be surrounded by alcohol, but I learned how to formulate a plan that would enable me to go and be with friends who drank. I would get a nonalcoholic beverage in my hand as soon as I arrived, focus on other things besides the booze, have an excuse ready for why I wasn't drinking, try to make conversations with people who did not breathe wine on me, and have an exit strategy for when I knew I needed to leave. I knew when it was time to go. I would start staring at that glass of wine, or martini, or whatever, just a few seconds too long. The drink devil sitting on my shoulder would start trying to tell me how good it would taste. That it would be okay if I just had one. Ha. Thank goodness that the tools I acquired in my recovery taught me better and prepared me for how to ignore this nonsense.

There are so many triggers for me. People, places, and things that I associate with drinking. I shared most of them in a piece I wrote called "Miss or Miss Out." Crabs with a cold pitcher of beer. Spicy Thai food paired with a cold glass of Viognier. Margaritas on Cinco de Mayo. Mint juleps at a Kentucky Derby party. A hearty Italian red wine with spaghetti and meatballs or lasagna. Cold beers at a tailgate at a concert or sporting event. Hot toddies after a day of skiing. A nice martini (with three olives) after a round of golf. I could go on, but right now, the trigger that's taking its aim at me is the beach. As beautiful as it is, and as much as I enjoy it, there are few things more challenging to my sobriety than coming up from the beach at the end of the day. The beach houses that surround me are filled with people enjoying their cocktails, cold beers, or blender drinks. It's like a Pavlovian response that's hard for me to break—that walk home from the beach, washing off the sand, and reaching for a cold drink of something yummy. To me, drinking was synonymous with the beach. Hell, drinking was synonymous with breathing, but right now we're talking about the beach.

It's one of those things I didn't think about until it whacked me like a crashing wave as I walked through the sand to go back to the house in the late afternoon on our first day at Fire Island. I actually said it out loud to my daughter, telling her that I forgot how much the beach made me crave a drink. Her incredibly thoughtful response was that we could go to the little general store and make some fun mocktails. Great idea. We did. And the craving passed. Sometimes just speaking it out loud takes the power out of a craving. Ice cream didn't hurt either.

The reminders of what the alternatives would be are also quite helpful. I've shared before that what often helps me the most is remembering to "think it all the way through." What happens after that first sip? In addition to throwing away my 2,612 days of sobriety and dealing with the shame and disappointment that would come with that, I know it wouldn't be just one sip. Or just one drink. It would be off to the races. And to a nasty hangover. And not being able to enjoy watching my sons jump in the waves. Or the beautiful sunset over the water. Or the serenity that I have gained in my sobriety.

So hopefully I can add the end of the day at the beach to my list of triggers that I am now better equipped to handle. There will be many more. But I will handle them like I do my days...one at a time.

"When we heal the wounds of our past, we move forward into our lives with an unburdened sense of self and a higher awareness of what our own triggers are." —Athena Laz

Roller Coaster or
Merry-Go-Round?

Today marks seven years and three months of sobriety. Two thousand six hundred forty-eight days. Three hundred seventy-eight weeks. What is significant about 2,648 days? Nothing. And everything. It represents 2,648 "one-day-at a-times." Countless victories over temptation and cravings and thoughts of giving in. Thousands of hours of work. Working through the ups of the "pink cloud" of sobriety, the downs of facing life on life's terms, and everything in between. Facing my darkest demons head-on and surviving the battles. Learning and understanding the true meaning of humility. Training myself to let go of things that are out of my control and turn them over to my Higher Power. Sometimes I take a moment to pat myself on the back. But I will face day 2,648 today as I do every other. Just for today, I will not pick up a drink. One day at a time.

I often hate dealing with life on life's terms. I still foolishly think I can do life on my terms. Never really works out, but I still try. I can honestly say that life is a zillion times better in sobriety than it was when I was drinking. But shit happens in life, whether you are stone-cold sober or numbing it out and fooling yourself into thinking you've found some sort of nirvana-like alternate reality. Life is hard. But life is beautiful. In these past seven years and three months, I have ridden the emotional roller coaster time and time again. Sobriety allows you to feel ineffable joy at times. It also gives you the presence to fully experience pain, hurt, sorrow, and grief—feelings that I often tried to avoid and numb by quickly reaching for the bottle. I can honestly say that I'd rather fully *feel* the joy and the sorrow than feel nothing.

There's a wonderful scene in the movie *Parenthood* with Steve Martin in which Grandma tells a story about riding on the roller coaster when she was younger. She said, "You know, it's just interesting to me that a ride could make me so frightened, so scared, so sick, so excited, and so thrilled all together. Some didn't like it. They went on the merry-go-round. That just goes around. Nothing. I like the roller coaster. You get more out of it." Steve Martin rolls his eyes thinking Grandma is just rambling. His wife, Mary Steen-burgen, clearly understands the wisdom that she is sharing with them. Life is much more like a roller coaster than a merry-go-round. Stay real.

Recently, my roller coaster ride included taking my oldest child to college. I see so many posts on social media about friends dropping their kids off at school. The excitement, the fear, and the sadness of them flying the coop, all captured in the pictures and posts. Many of these kids I've known since they were babies. How did this happen? It honestly feels like just yesterday that I was taking my daughter to the playground to play with them. But time flies, kids grow, and they move on. I didn't cry. I was so thrilled that she seemed happy, grounded, and ready to go. I realized that's the best I could ask for as a parent. To prepare them to move on and be strong on their own, teach them to make smart decisions, and always listen to and trust their gut.

When I drank, I couldn't trust my gut. I couldn't hear my gut. And I know, beyond the shadow of a doubt, that being present and available for my kids is a true gift of sobriety. Whether I am at the top of the roller coaster, about to experience that thrill of the drop, or at the bottom, working slowly on the climb up, I am here for them. Fully present. Fully feeling.

The heat of the summer is coming to an end. The leaves will start falling and another season will arrive. Mother Nature's roller coaster. We will put the bathing suits, swim goggles, and pool bags away and get out our new gear, sport our kids' school colors, and cheer at their football and lacrosse games. We will share in their triumphs and disappointments. We won't make them stay on the merry-go-round. We will let them ride the roller coaster. But we will buckle them in and let them know they are loved. And tell them to enjoy the ride.

> *"Raising children who are hopeful and who have the courage to be vulnerable means stepping back and letting them experience disappointment, deal with conflict, learn how to assert themselves, and have the opportunity to fail. If we're always following our children into the arena, hushing the critics, and assuring their victory, they'll never learn that they have the ability to dare greatly on their own."*
> —Brené Brown, *Daring Greatly*

The Sobrietease Manifesto

If I can remember to focus on some basic things, I can stay sober, one day at a time.

Just for today, **I will not pick up a drink**.

I will turn my will and my life over to my Higher Power.

I will continue to look at my faults and my defects of character and make amends to those whom I have hurt or wronged.

There is no problem that a drink cannot make worse.

When I think about picking up a drink, I have to remember to **think it all the way through.**

My life is so much better sober than when I drank.

I'd rather feel both the joy and the pain than feel nothing. Life is a roller coaster ride. Be present for the ups and downs and all that goes with them.

Alcoholism is a disease. It is not something I asked for. It is not something that can be cured by a doctor or a magic pill. It is not a weakness or lack of will power. It is a disease.

I am not alone. I can always reach out to another alcoholic who understands and doesn't judge.

I can reach out to friends who may not have the disease but who care and love me and want to help. I can *always* turn to my Higher Power.

I have a choice about whether or not I pick up a drink. Once I pick up a drink, the drink makes the choice for me.

Sobriety is a gift. It is a daily reprieve, contingent upon the maintenance of my spiritual condition.

In order to **FLY**, you must **F**irst **L**ove **Y**ourself.

I can say the Serenity Prayer over, and over, and over again whenever I need to.

I can start my day over at any point.

I learned how to speak my truth, and speak it with grace.

I discovered the power of gratitude.

I learned that I can write. And that sharing my experience, strength, and hope can, and does, help others.

God, grant me the serenity to accept the things I cannot change, the courage to change the things I can, and the wisdom to know the difference.

And, God, grant me the serenity to laugh at life...

About the Author

 Martha Carucci is an author and blogger who lives in Alexandria, Virginia, with her husband and three children. She spent many years as a lobbyist for the telecommunications industry and is currently the Executive Director of the National Breast Center Foundation. She studied at the University of Pennsylvania, Harvard, and Georgetown.

Martha has appeared on numerous television and radio shows, including *Great Day Washington, The Dee Armstrong Show, The Chad Benson Show,* and *The Mike Schikman Show.* Her writing has been featured in many publications, including the *Chicago Sun Times, BrazenWoman.com, WomenYouShouldKnow.com,* and *The Tamed Cynic.* She speaks to various groups and audiences about alcoholism and her recovery, and was recently featured on the popular podcast *We Should Talk About That* in an episode titled "Alcohol, Sobriety and the Journey in Between." Martha was awarded the City of Alexandria Commission for Women's "Women's Health and Safety Advocate Award." She is an avid golfer and tennis player, and active volunteer in the community.

Martha's first book, *Sobrietease,* was the #1 New Release on Amazon for Alcoholism and Recovery. She continues to publish writing on her blog, and is currently working on a novel.

Visit Martha's blog *Sobrietease* at sobrietease.wordpress.org

 @sobrieteaseblog

 @Sobrietease